The Iron Goddess Code:

A Lifelong Journey of Hidden Mindfuck and Relationship Warfare to a Fierce New Freedom

The Iron Goddess Code:
A LIFELONG JOURNEY OF HIDDEN MINDFUCK AND RELATIONSHIP WARFARE TO A FIERCE NEW FREEDOM

KATHY BRODEUR

StoryTerrace

Text Michele Vrouvas, on behalf of StoryTerrace

Design Grade Design and Adeline Media, London

Copyright © Kathy Brodeur and StoryTerrace

Text is private and confidential

First Print January 2021

StoryTerrace

www.StoryTerrace.com

CONTENTS

PROLOGUE: FEELING CLOSE

Some years ago, I was finishing up a breezy luncheon with a good friend, when the conversation turned to the chaos in my marriage. My husband's infidelity, his all-nighters, the emotional abuse I'd endured for much too long.

We were at a trendy cafe in St. Catharines in Ontario, Canada. My friend listened attentively. When I was done talking, she took a deep breath, looked me in the eye, and shook her head gently.

"Kathy," she said. "*Where* is your self-respect?"

To this day, I can feel the sting of those words. Yes, my marriage had seen turbulence, but it hadn't eaten away at my core. I was still the same person, easygoing, upbeat, self-assured.

Wasn't I?

Truth is, my friend's question threw me off my game, made me think. What kind of life had I been living, and more importantly, why?

Thus began my journey to self. It took some time and a few false starts, but I came to realize that there was no way for me to move on until I moved out.

Which brings me to this book. I am writing not out of resentment or the desire for payback against my husband, but from an urge to let others in similar situations know there is a way out. Abuse is never acceptable.

Reader, you might see yourself in my story. The vows you made to yourself, to love him unconditionally and so to transform him into a caring and empathetic husband, only to find that even unconditional love has its limits.

If so, know that I walked in your shoes until I reached the end of the road, my road yes, but perhaps also yours.

This book tells how I lost myself in a narcissistic marriage until a series of wake-up calls pushed me to learn about the widespread disorder known as narcissism and to discover that I was not alone. Had such a book been around 25 years ago, I would've had the knowledge and power to discard the mindfuck of a marriage that I am now terminating. Before we go any further, however, I need to emphasize one overarching point: I am not certified to diagnose my ex nor, to my knowledge, has he been diagnosed as a narcissist. However, the similarities between his behaviors and characteristics are alarmingly similar to those of narcissists. I am encouraging my readers to hear me out and judge for themselves.

My story does not offer tidy resolutions; no Cinderella endings. My divorce has not been finalized, nor am I yet sufficiently distanced from my abuser.

I know that healing is possible, and it awaits me if I can learn to love myself once again. I am not there yet. But I'm feeling very close, and right now very close is good enough for me.

***

"When I was a little girl, I used to read fairy tales. In fairy tales, you meet Prince Charming, and he's everything you ever wanted. In fairy tales, the bad guy is very easy to spot. The bad guy is always wearing a black cape, so you always know who he is. Then you grow up, and you realize that Prince Charming is not as easy to find as you thought. You realize the bad guy is not wearing a black cape, and he's not easy to spot; he's really funny, and he makes you laugh, and he has perfect hair."

—Singer Taylor Swift, introducing her song "White Horse"

1

AWAKE

"What's going on in your life?"

Robert was about to start my facial when he noticed a few outbreaks of acne dotted across my skin. This wasn't completely out of the ordinary for me. Acne would occasionally make an appearance here and there, but on this particular day Robert noticed it was accompanied by severe inflammation. He was immediately concerned.

"Oh, the usual. Stress!" I said, probably with a shrug, maybe even a laugh.

But Robert wasn't laughing. He had done my facials for the past fifteen years. It took just one quick glance at my skin for him to know that something was up.

I started to tell him about the marriage. Brian went out *a lot*, drinking heavily with friends, doing God knows what with God knows who, then fielding my questions the next morning with lies, half-truths, stories up the wazoo. If I was feeling gutsy, I might push back, pointing out inconsistencies in his story. But that would only serve to unleash any number of hostile reactions. So most times, at least during the first decade or two, I wasn't feeling up to the battle. Brian would just wave off my hurt and confusion and roll himself into bed, usually after 6 a.m., to sleep the day away. The whole episode would blow over until the next skirmish, which most often was just a few days away.

Robert thought for a second and then said, "Oh, so he's a narcissist."

Narcissist? Of course I was familiar with the word. I knew it was used in reference to self-absorbed, loud, and obnoxious people. I had no idea it was a term for behavior that had anything to do with my marriage.

I decided to do some research and dive a little deeper into this personality disorder. I discovered that there are a few different types of narcissists. The term overt narcissist refers to loud, self-absorbed, and arrogant people. The overt narc is not a sympathetic character. When challenged, he will rage and insist that his needs be catered to immediately. He is very dangerous and also very obvious.

The term *covert narcissist* is the opposite of the overt narc. He is hidden and operates in secret. He is perhaps even more dangerous because of the way he doesn't allow the outside world to see the truth that the victim sees. Covert narcs are charming and always willing to help anyone who can help them, which means they always have an agenda.

The covert narc can be extremely hard to spot. You always feel that something about them isn't quite right. By the time you figure it out, the damage has been done. Covert narcs are unassuming, so even a lot of professionals have difficulty spotting them. This type comes off as very trustworthy and pretends to have the best interest of others at heart, but there is always an agenda. The covert narc sounds like the personality of my ex to a tee.

I continued to research. The end game of any kind of narcissist is the same: aggressive, callous, and cunning actions; a complete absence of conscience and empathy. This type is a pretender and can cry at the drop of a hat. In that regard, my ex was an Emmy-winning performer with deceptive ability to behave in superficially charming ways while hiding purely selfish motives. This type has a willingness to use intimidation and violence to control others in order to satisfy their own needs while having a complete absence of guilt or remorse. They know how to shift blame, to accuse others of what they are guilty of. They also have no accountability for any of their actions, and they engage in pathological lying, gaslighting using denial, lying, misinformation, and contradiction to make you doubt your memory perception and change reality to suit their lies. They're good at guilt tripping, silent treatment projections, throwing tantrums, and bullying when a victim speaks his truth. This type thinks they can bully you into being quiet and not questioning them or their behavior. Negative humor and making negative remarks disguised as sarcasm or humor to make you feel inferior, pretend ignorance, and playing dumb in order to get away with bad behavior are other behaviors. The covert narc needs revenge, shows passive-aggressive characteristics, and can't handle any type of criticism.

That's quite a list, I know, but these people are so unhappy with themselves that they are out to destroy their victim, the person who makes them thrive.

***

"If a man hates himself, he takes it out on the woman who loves him."

***

Now, I would like to make one thing very clear: my ex was not diagnosed with narcissism. Nor am I in a position to certifiably make that diagnosis. However, the similarities of the typical narcissistic personality disorder and my ex are too palpable to ignore.

Robert is probably one the smartest humans I have ever had the pleasure of knowing. Not only does he study human behavior as a hobby, but he and his family have also had the displeasure of having a narcissist in their family circle, as well. Again, I will stress, although Robert is not technically certified to make such a diagnosis, he too noticed the striking resemblances between a textbook narcissist and my ex's behavior over the years.

You, reader, can come to your own conclusion at the end of this book.

I would like to add that I have started and restarted and rewrote the content and structure of this book during many phases of my healing from emotional abuse. I believe I have come to a higher level for providing events and information. I have tried to keep details down to a minimum so as to allow you to read between the lines. This will save my children the embarrassment of knowing all the terrible events. It is not up to me to convince my children or anyone else who my ex truly is. The truth will reveal itself eventually because one gets tired of carrying on a fake persona.

2

LA LA LAND

They were always right there, staring me in the face. The red flags. There since the day that Brian and I first laid eyes on each other at the food court at Pen Centre in St. Catharines.

He was buying gifts for his then girlfriend. "Let me introduce you two," said the guy who was with Brian, someone I kind of knew. I took one look at Brian's dark hair, blue eyes, incredibly buff body and felt my heart jump. I noticed too that he was into my bubbly personality and big blonde curls.

That night, while babysitting, I was on the phone with a friend. "He's sooooo cute," I told her. She was dating one of Brian's friends and was able to get Brian's number. I could tell he was happy that I called. He was heading out to a party that night and asked me to call him the next day. I did, and we talked for six straight hours.

I was fifteen and in the tenth grade. He was seventeen and a senior at a different school. His house was a fifteen minute drive from mine.

Things between us got intense, fast. We saw a lot of each other, spent hours on the phone each night. Brian's background seemed solid. He came from a good family. He was a good student who excelled at high school football and basketball. He was shy and quiet. He seemed like a great catch.

Our dates were over-the-top romantic. He took me ice skating, to drive-ins, and parties. He was lots of fun and treated me like a lady, holding the door open and showing me total respect.

He was a charmer, for sure. So charming, in fact, that I sidelined some early red flags. One was Brian's reputation for heavy drinking and hearty partying. He started drinking at a very young age. By all accounts, too, he was a social animal, hanging with lots of girls and guys who were a mix of good and terrible. Some had sketchy reputations. Some had even been to jail.

Once, Brian went to a high school dance with his friend. I did not find out until after the event and only because Brian's friend with the big mouth told me. Knowing his friend had blabbed, Brian rushed to cover his ass. "She wanted me to dance with her," he said. "I couldn't hurt her feelings." In other words, he wasn't cheating on me. He was performing a noble deed, dancing with a girl to avoid hurting her feelings. But what about mine?

That, by the way, was an excuse Brian would use countless times, in countless similar and other situations, over the entire relationship.

Another time, early in the relationship, he asked me to come to his house. I wanted to look my best, so I spent a little extra time on my clothes and makeup, probably arriving later than he'd expected. After I had been there for a while, Brian said he and a friend needed to step out. Someone they knew, a bouncer at a strip joint, had been shot and killed. Off they went, Brian and his friend, to "console" their buddies at a time of need. I mean, it was all on the up-and-up, right? What else would two cool dudes be doing at a strip joint?

Me, I was ditched. I now see that little play by Brian as his need to control me and our get-togethers. He wasn't just going out with friends. His message was: "We're not doing this now. I will deal with you later." It worked then and thousands of times thereafter.

Meanwhile, Brian's behind-the-scenes antics showed no sign of stopping. On Wednesdays, he went with his buddies to ladies' night. It was a snowy Thursday morning when I was on a bus headed down a main street. I spotted Brian's car parked at a triplex where I knew another girl lived. I am sure that I asked him about it. I do not remember his response, but I will bet my last dollar that it was just another lie.

I was miffed by these indiscretions, but I brushed each one aside. I didn't want to overreact. I was naive and inexperienced; I never had many boyfriends, so I had no idea what was and wasn't acceptable behavior for guys in exclusive relationships. I certainly didn't want to come across as a bitch who was restricting a seventeen-year-old from his dude time.

On top of all that, when Brian was good, he was head-in-the-clouds romantic. For our first night together, he bought me silver wine goblets. Other times, he'd cook me a gourmet dinner, treat me to champagne, expensive chocolate, and strawberries. In bed, he made sure that I was completely satisfied. He made the whole night about me. Brian was a gifted seducer. He knew exactly which buttons to push and how to expertly push each one. No doubt about it, I was swept off my feet.

Schmoozed is the word that now comes to mind. Brian schmoozed not only me but my mom, too. In fact, I was never able to convince Mom that Brian wasn't the person he presented himself to be, at least not until the last few years. Throughout the marriage, I would bring up instances of Brian's carousing behavior or his deceptions. "Oh, Kathy," Mom would say, with a wave of her hand and look on her face that implied I was blowing things way out of proportion. Like almost every other decent person who had come into contact with Brian, Mom had put him on a pedestal. To her, he was a shy, quiet, awesome human being, nothing at all like the cunning and heartless manipulator who was pulling my strings.

***

The points I am about to make about the *La La Land* stage must be tempered by this admission: I am not certified to diagnose my ex as a narcissist and, to my knowledge, no one else has diagnosed him as such. I am merely explaining that the similarities between his behaviors and characteristics are alarmingly similar to those of narcissists. Readers, please consider the following statements and come to your own conclusions.

***

La La Land refers to the initial stage of a narcissistic relationship. Some psychologists also use the term "blind and deaf" to describe the early stage when a narcissist doubles down on charm and charisma solely to lure prospective partners. The narcissistic man presents himself as confident, charming, and grandiose. These types are most often high achievers with above-average intelligence and varied talents, both physical and social. Others see only the carefully constructed persona that the narcissist has taken pains to orchestrate.

Once the prospect is lured in, the narcissist's sugar-coating persuasion kicks into high gear. They use sweet talk to manipulate their partner's emotions. They use their sexual prowess to arouse lust. However, although this period sees high levels of intense sexual activity, true emotional intimacy is often lacking or non-existent.

"On cloud nine" is how many women have described their feelings at this stage. Being with the narcissist has flooded them with passion, energy, and desire. The narcissist uses flattery, gifts, and sexual pleasures to make women feel special, but it is only to get what he wants. Some women recall having initially questioned their husband's "too good to be true" demeanor. Most, however, admit they were powerless to resist.

For the woman, La La Land is a time of rapture. One woman described her feelings at this stage as follows: "I was so falling in love with this guy. It was a dreamy time. One day, I was just walking down the street, and a truck driver leaned out of his window and yelled to me, 'Hey lady! What's the secret? Why are you so happy?'"

Yes, La La Land is enchanting, but it doesn't last. When women return to earth, they begin to notice an imbalance in the narcissist's personality and behavior, and striking differences between them that should not go unnoticed.

Unfortunately, most women do not return to earth until after the wedding. They got through the courtship by overlooking a number of red flags: his tendency to control them, to have a wandering eye, and flirtatious spirit; to show no real concern for his fiancé, her future, her time. No doubt they have also dismissed the concerns of friends and family who can see more clearly the destructive path the woman now blindly follows. Even if the woman entertains warnings of friends and family, she is more likely than not all too quick to rationalize and suppress them.

He loves me, and I love him. Love is all we need. This is the mantra she repeats to no end. Some women admit to going as far as telling themselves that when problems do arise, inevitably, the couple's love is strong enough to keep things together. They will work through the conflict, doing whatever needs to be done. Such is the degree of commitment a woman in love with a narcissist is likely to have and to think is mutual. But in reality she has no reason to believe her future husband will work through any problem between them. Up to this point, he has never shown any signs of empathy or respect for her feelings, or even emotional engagement in the relationship. In reality, this way of thinking brings to light the woman's undiscerning mindset. She really has no idea what she's getting herself into.

La La Land leads many women down the aisle. But once they tie the knot and get to see the man behind the mask—a man easily provoked to anger and manipulative in every way—there is extreme regret for not having listened to their intuition and called the wedding off.

An anecdote in a best-selling book on narcissism tells the story of a woman on her wedding day. Her father knows that his daughter has second thoughts about the man she is going to marry. Minutes before the father and bride are about to begin the procession into the church, the father pulls her aside. "Just say the word," he tells her, "and I will go right into that church and tell every one of those guests that no way is my daughter going to marry that man. You can take my car keys and drive far away and never have to face any of them. I will gladly do that for you. Just give me the word." The bride paused for a moment but couldn't muster the courage.

She did come to regret that decision. Of course, by then it was too late. She was already trapped in the turbulent marriage, shaking her head and asking, *How did I not see this coming?*

3

A MOTHER PROBLEM

"Narcissism has its roots in childhood." That was the lead of an article I read in the process of researching for this book. It brought me back to my very first conversation with Brian.

He stopped talking abruptly and yelled at the top of his lungs, "*I hate you, you f—ing cow!*"

"Who in the world are you talking to?" I asked.

"Oh, my mother," he said, "and I'm only joking."

I didn't learn the real story until much later. Not only was Brian's mother not home that day, but he also wasn't joking. He made that random outburst knowing his mother wasn't around to hear it, knowing he was safe.

This begs the question: Why on earth would he do such a thing?

I have a theory. His outburst was a way to release pent-up anger against a woman whom he considered to be a mother in name only.

This is totally in keeping with other things I learned about Brian's rather rough childhood. I knew his family was intact and that his father was a beautiful little Frenchman, a quiet and peaceful man who was overpowered by his louder and more domineering wife.

Shelby bullied her kids with her words and sometimes even her fists. Their relationship didn't mellow in the coming years. They were never close. Despite the emotional disconnect that he's never denied, Brian now says that he loves his mother. That may be true, but there have been many other times when his sentiments about her were much darker. Like near the end of our daughter Carly's wedding reception, when the party was over and guests were restless to leave, but Shelby insisted on speaking. She launched into a drawn-out talk about nothing in particular, her only intention to grab the spotlight. Later, in the hotel room when he was a bit drunk, Brian said he was mortified at her public display.

Knowing about Brian's mother problem broke my heart. It also had a too-powerful influence on my reactions to him since day one. I pitied him, and that probably is one of the reasons I stayed so long. I remember thinking, *This poor thing, he grew up never feeling real love. So how could I expect him to show it? What examples from his childhood did he have to draw back on?*

What did Brian's mother problem have to do with our marriage? Plenty.

"Your issues aren't with me," I'd tell him, "your real problem is with your mother."

Instinctively, he'd shoot that idea down, but I have come to learn that it is not far-fetched by any means. In fact, when I researched the causes of narcissistic personalities, most experts linked them to childhood abuse and neglect, which robs people of empathy, and prevents them from showing—or even feeling—real love.

***

The psychology literature abounds with examples of narcissistic men who had terrible relationships with their mothers. It's called *childhood emotional neglect* (CEN), and it refers to children growing up unseen and unheard. Their emotional needs are neglected, their feelings never tapped into by parents, mostly mothers, who are indifferent and controlling. CEN has long-term effects that are serious enough to leave a child with an emotional vacuum.

I read about narcissists who went out of their way in public to show total respect for women. But behind closed doors, their behavior was anything but well-mannered. Hooking up with strippers, having extra-marital affairs, and carrying on at seedy bars are all behaviors these men engage in, reflecting their deep-seated resentment toward a mother with whom they did not bond.

A mother who bullied them, who challenged their masculinity when it was still in its formative stage of development, disrupting the natural maturation of a healthy self-image, is also one reason that narcissists turn to strippers and prostitutes. Sex for these men becomes a purely physical act, devoid of feelings. Strippers and prostitutes are hired hands who must do as they are told. The narcissist holds the reins. He is in total control. He calls the shots, forcing them to submit in the most self-effacing ways; in effect, treating them with the cruel indifference with which he never had the courage to treat his own mother.

The narcissist with mother problems never develops the hearty self-esteem necessary to forge lasting relationships based on trust and respect. As a result, he never learns to function properly in a family. These men do not develop the ability to entertain other viewpoints or connect with others, to feel what others are feeling.

When confronted about having a mother problem, these men often resort to denial. Rather than work through the tangle of emotions caused by an abusive mother, they prefer instead to go on believing that their tormented childhood circumstances did not exist.

Once again, I am reminding the reader that I am not qualified to state that my ex is or ever was a narcissist. I have no information that any professional has given him this diagnosis. What I am saying here is that the similarities of the classic narcissist are quite similar to those exhibited by my ex. The reader is now left to her own judgments.

4

I LOVE THAT YOU'RE SO NAIVE

will never forget Brian saying those words to me, and I will never forget my response: "Really? So you love how friggin' stupid I am?"

Stupid's too strong a word, I now understand. It had nothing to do with me being stupid. It had everything to do with me trusting my husband, the father of my children, the man whom I loved without condition, and being ready at any moment to push aside my intuition, that steady inner voice telling me he was once again up to no good.

Inexperienced is another good word and describes me to a tee. I was a babe in the woods when I met Brian and stayed that way through much of the marriage. Very early on, Brian had sized that up beautifully. He could tell that the closest I had ever come to bad behavior or even teenage rebellion was telling an occasional lie to my parents and smoking one cigarette in the ninth grade. My idea of a good time was going to the Sunday matinee with a friend. Oh yes, from the very beginning Brian had wisely calculated that I was no match for his cunning.

That is how, through our entire lives together, Brian wormed his way out of one compromising situation after another. It explains why friends and relatives now ask whether I knew all along what Brian was really up to all those weekends, vacations, and nights when he was safely out of my sight. That's how obvious it was to everyone but me.

The examples are endless. Like the time I was five months pregnant with Carly. I invited Brian's mom and sister to dinner but made sure to check with Brian first.

"You're playing football at ten o'clock that morning," I reminded him. "Dinner will be at five. Does that give you enough time?" I asked.

"Of course," he said.

"Are you sure you're gonna be home?" With Brian, I always had to spell things out. The less wiggle room the better.

"Yes, yes," he insisted, "I'm going to be home!"

So the day arrived, Brian's mom and sister showed up, dinner was on the table, five o'clock came . . . and went. No Brian. Thirty minutes later, I was calling his cell and getting no answer. A little more time passed before I reached out to Brian's friend. "Nope, he's not with me," he said. So I tried someone else, the wife of a friend, and finally I found out where "they" were. I drove to the location she gave me and sure enough, Brian's car was outside and he was in a bar, hanging out with some buddies, all of them hammered.

Had I not been so naive, I would never have given him the benefit of the doubt, telling myself that guys playing football are bound to lose track of time. No, I would have immediately perceived what really went down: Brian had no intention of being home on time. He had arranged for friends to lie and throw me off the track. Had I not been so naive, I would not have let the whole thing blow over with his simple, "Just having a good time with the guys, Kathy!"

My naiveté is what explains Brian getting away with missing the kids' Christmas concerts at school, Carly' s dance recitals, Greg's Saturday morning hockey practice. He had been partying until 6:00 a.m. the next morning.

It was how Brian twisted his way out of a dicey situation in 2017, when I really thought I had caught him red-handed. He had gone to Bali with a friend. One night when he was at the bar he pocket dialed me, and I got to hear my husband discussing a transaction relating to "party supplies and entertainment." That one must have been a real doozy. Brian had gone out of his way to cover every base, not even telling his friend, who remained just as clueless as I was about Brian's shady little move that night. He had managed to feign sickness and slink away, leaving his buddy at the bar, while Brian secretly returned to his hotel room to something I don't even want to imagine.

In that same call, I heard Brian discussing another trip he had taken to Curacao. I remembered that trip. That was the time his phone went dead on a Saturday night. How unbelievably convenient, I thought. Here I was, thousands of miles away, powerless to prove that his excuse later on—"It was an accident, I swear!"—was in fact another big, fat lie.

When Brian was back home from Bali, he had a bottle of herbal Viagra in which exactly four pills—only one dose—were missing. He blew past that one without even blinking an eye. "Oh, Keith and I took some on the way home from the airport, just for kicks, just to see how it would make us feel!" When he noticed my raised eyebrow and blank glare, he must have sensed that I did not believe he and Keith didn't go drinking or partying after taking the pills. So he shot back with another of his favorite lines: "If you do not believe me, just ask Keith!" Of course, "asking Keith" was another roadblock. These guys were all joined at the hip, primed to cover each other, stay true to their motto of "bros before hoes."

Over time, Brian's excuses did more than render me speechless. They actually conditioned me to believe I was overreacting. Every time I heard "Kathy, you're way too sensitive" or "Stop making a big deal about nothing," I was once again that wide-eyed teenager, afraid to make waves, to reel in her happy-go-lucky boyfriend who was just sowing his oats, having a little bro time. The conditioning created a dangerous mindset in which the slightest raising of Brian's voice had me backing down pronto. Funny how I don't even remember being conscious of having that mindset. But Brian sure was.

It allowed him to dial down my anger until it was nothing more than a gentle simmer, just the right temperature for him to swoop in with another round of love bombing. Pricey wine, expensive gifts, sex, you name it, anything to make me forget the bad and remember only the good, to renew my belief that, no matter his indiscretion, we would be okay, somehow, some day. On went the cycle of abuse.

Yes, Brian was really that smooth, that calculating. He had not only me but almost every single acquaintance of ours believing he was Mr. Wonderful. I learned early on that it was futile to confide my doubts about him to our friends. "Kathy, no way," they would tell me, "you've got to be wrong. Brian loves you. He can't stop bragging about you!"

The few people who weren't fooled by Brian remained silent, believing there was no need to tell me because I was already fully aware of his goings on. People like my brother who, years later, summed it up best: "Wow, Kathy, it was just so obvious, he was doing it right under your nose. I assumed you were okay with it."

The "it" he was referring to was Brian's affair with Mary, who once was a friend of mine. Their hookup happened about ten years into our marriage, and it was one of the first wake-up calls for me.

Until then, Brian stepped out whenever the spirit took him, knowing the consequences were nil. His gullible wife was walking in step. My naiveté explains how Visa statements with suspicious charges and pocket-dialed conversations were saying one thing, and Brian was insisting on quite another. Events happened right under my nose, and Brian was able to convince me that I wasn't seeing things that were as plain as day. It was how he got away with tugging on the pants of a waitress at the end of a boat cruise, with me *right there.*

"Oh, c'mon," he said, "I was just joking!" Sad but true. And to think that I fell for it. Every. Single. Time.

***

"Great sex and the right lies will make a person waste years of their lives."

***

Labeling someone as a narcissist is a serious claim to make. I am not qualified to label my ex—or anyone else, for that matter—as a narcissist. To my knowledge, my ex has never been diagnosed as such. My statements in this chapter are intended only to compare the behavior and characteristics exhibited by my ex with those of the classic narcissist as described by professionals. I will leave my readers to consider these statements and judge for themselves.

Narcissists are known to prey on the innocent. Narcissistic men are adept at choosing kind and sensitive women whom they perceive as vulnerable. A mild-mannered woman who prefers to avoid confrontation at all costs is a character trait too appealing for the narcissistic man to overlook. Such a woman is considered to be a perfect match. She is the "empty vessel" who can be molded into the ideal partner for a man who craves the spotlight.

But, in time, the woman is bound to recognize a pattern. There is a gap between what these men say and what they do. If the woman musters the courage to voice concern, question motives or behavior, the narcissist resorts to a particular form of psychological abuse known as *gaslighting*. Psychology blogs are filled with true stories of naive women who, for incredibly long periods of time, were duped by a narcissistic husband.

Then the day arrives. Something happens to shed light. The woman walks in on a compromising exchange between her husband and another woman. Or she overhears the shamelessly flirtatious tone he uses on the phone with a colleague. Perhaps she is sitting in the booth next to him as his eyes devour the pretty, young thing who is taking his order for a burger and "whatever nice shake" comes with that. She speaks up. What did he mean? Why is he holding her hand? Did he really have to ask if her husband was home?

Thus confronted, the narcissist resorts to gaslighting. This is a diversionary tactic that is designed to make the wife question her sense of reality and adopt her husband's. What she saw, he tells her, she really didn't see. Or she did not understand what she heard him say. *No, dear, I am sorry to tell you that you are hopelessly clueless, so f—ing naive.*

Gaslighting distorts reality for the victim and deflects responsibility away from the narcissist. Start with a woman who is by nature naive and trusting. Go at her with dumbfounded expressions, a shake of the head, and phrases like "What are you talking about? You know I would never do that," and you end up with an alternative version of the facts and a victim feeling overwhelming defeat. Gaslighting is one handy tool in the narcissist's chest. It is highly effective. It works like a charm.

5

WITH MY BEST FRIEND

Early in the relationship, a friend shared with me her first impression of Brian: "He is open to any *and every* opportunity."

It was not what I wanted to hear, but Brian's all-too-frequent indiscretions made it hard to deny. There was the time before we were engaged that he slept with a girl on the football team. When I found out, I thought about calling off the wedding. Then I remembered the enormous effort of invitations, venues, food, all those guests who would be so disappointed. I couldn't go through with it. Part of me also wanted to believe Brian's excuse: "The guys challenged me to do it. I didn't want to. I would never do that to you."

Of course, now I know that would have been the best time to say, "That is the end. I'm out!"

But it was too painful to process the hurt, so I allowed my heart to do all the talking, drowning out the suspicions flooding my brain. I loved Brian deeply. I did not want to believe he was capable of infidelity. I made a conscious decision to take the moral high ground. Rather than confront him with his questionable conduct, I would quietly lead by example. Show him patience, understanding, loyalty, and love. That was sure to get his notice and to make him change his tune.

I developed that mindset early on in the marriage, when Brian got into a habit of not coming home on Wednesday and Sunday nights. He would play football and then party at Bill and Mary's house until six o'clock the next morning.

Bill and Mary were our close friends. I considered Mary to be my best friend and confided in her often. Did it bother me that Brian was spending so many nights away from home, even if he was with two people whom I trusted? Yes and no. I did have passing thoughts that such frequent and lengthy absences could mean he was misbehaving. Then again, I knew where he was and with whom. If I even hinted that untoward things were going on, Brian was quick to shoot it down with a challenge that seemed irreproachable: "I was at Bill's house all night. Just ask Mary!"

These weekly gatherings went on for many years, until the day that Mary got angry. She began to spill her guts. She sent Brian running for cover.

I first noticed a change in her behavior when she and I were together. She would get drunk and say strange things. "Brian and I have such a good connection," she said to me out of the blue. "We connect in *so many* great ways."

The emphatic tone nagged at me. I found her choice of words a bit strong, but I am by nature non-confrontational and decided it was not worth pursuing.

She didn't let up and started to toss out more serious allegations. She might have started at the incidental, but she was now going for the jugular.

"I'm screwing your husband," she blurted out during an otherwise perfectly casual visit. You want to talk about being frozen with fear? I did not—could not—react immediately. My goal was to remain calm. I might even have thought I heard wrong. I am pretty sure that the room started to darken, and I went kind of numb.

Around this time, I'd been seeing a therapist, Dr. Jordan. Brian had convinced me not to mention Mary's outburst during a therapy session. He said it would only make me look bad. Mary said the same thing, although at a different time, when Brian wasn't around.

I now realize what a lame excuse that was. Instead of saving me from an embarrassing situation with Dr. Jordan, it was designed to prevent Dr. Jordan from figuring out what those two were doing behind my back.

In the coming days, it was hard not to think about Mary's drunken words. The more I thought, the more images came to mind, the way Brian and Mary behaved when they thought no one was looking. There was the body language between them that I noticed from a distance. I was reading between the lines, so I guess it was obvious where my mind was going. I had no idea and certainly not a shred of proof. All I had to go on were snippets of events. One in particular was a pool party at our house. I walked into the rec room and walked in on Mary and Brian. They were having a moment. The music was loud, but I was sure I heard her say, "Oh, come on, Brian, you're chicken."

Stunned, I backed out of the room and didn't mention it until everyone had gone. Brian admitted that Mary said that, but of course, he said I was foolish to give it any thought. "She was trying to pull me into the shower with her," he said, "but I didn't do it." Then I remembered the shower tap had been broken, and my thoughts took off like a rocket. *OMG! Would they, did they f—k in the shower?* The blood rushed to my head. I could feel my heart pound.

What I did next is still kind of a blur. More than likely, I accepted whatever might have happened between them. I was still reeling from a personal crisis of my own and lacked the emotional fortitude to fully accept that my husband had been cheating on me with my own best friend. I did not push the issue any further with Brian. As far as Mary was concerned, I distanced myself from her and ended our friendship, a move that Brian found "harsh." Until, that is, Mary turned on him.

I was not there when it happened, but I noticed the friendship among those three had taken a peculiar turn. Brian stopped going to their house. He pulled back from Bill and stopped relying on Mary for alibis.

I found out later that Mary had become a loose cannon, drinking like a sailor and making all kinds of noise. Brian kind of freaked out. If he wasn't careful, things might get back to me. Mary was no longer his trusted friend, the useful pawn. Maybe she did it hoping they would end up together. Maybe she did it to right a wrong Brian had committed against her. Whatever the reason, she made a fatal mistake. She crossed a line and became Public Enemy Number One.

I understand that people make mistakes. I told Brian that if there was something I needed to know, he should feel free to be completely honest with me. I was willing to listen and to avoid judgment and to work through whatever came our way. However, he never did show any accountability for his actions during this or any other time.

***

Chronic infidelity is a trademark of the narcissistic personality type, probably owing to the lack of self-control these people exhibit. They are unwilling and unable to tamp down their whims. A narcissist wants what he wants and when he wants it.

An extramarital fling feeds both the narcissist's appetite for sex and his desire for worship. These men know they are masters of the bedroom. They revel in their sexual abilities and cannot resist the urge to flaunt them. Some of this urge is fueled—unknowingly—by their wives who cannot hide their ecstasy, who praise their husband's skill at pressing all the right buttons. Puffed up, the narcissist savors these high points. If his wife is bowled over by his talents in bed, why not spread the talent around and enjoy more adulation?

Narcissistic men do not feel constrained by the conventions of long-term relationships or marriage. They cheat because they can and because the naive women they choose to marry make it easy for them to indulge their extramarital urges whenever they like.

Narcissists cheat because they are unable to feel regret or guilt, thus they never come face to face with negative emotions. They do not value the traditional moral traits of honesty and integrity. The narcissistic husband is accountable only to himself. So long as his needs are met, the end justifies the means. To the victor belong the spoils.

Infidelity makes perfect sense to a man who shuns the idea that he is accountable to his wife. This goes beyond owning up to one's mistakes. It goes to the narcissist's core belief that he is perfect and above reproach.

Lack of accountability is a byproduct of this personality type's lack of empathy. Think about it. What thoughts serve to deter a partner who is tempted to stray from the relationship? Usually, it is the partner's ability to see themselves in someone else's shoes. One woman described to her therapist how empathy played a role in her decision not to cheat. "I couldn't do that to my husband. He might not be perfect, but then again, neither am I. I can just imagine how hurt I'd be to find out he was with another woman. I didn't want to inflict that pain on him. He didn't deserve it. That is what stopped me from having the fling."

But to a personality who entertains no one's view but his, empathetic sentiments have no role in decision-making. They lack empathy. They will never tune in to their partners' emotions. They will never consider their partners' feelings because they do not matter.

Helping the narcissist to outmaneuver his partner are individuals known as "flying monkeys." These people enable the narcissist to concoct dirty schemes. They provide alibis and cover. They do so either because they derive some benefit from the narcissist's deception or just for the cheap thrill.

For the narcissist, the most desirable type of flying monkey is one who holds as much risk in the deception as the narcissist. That is why these men say they prefer to have affairs with married women who have just as much to lose as they do.

The devious plan rolls along smoothly as long as the flying monkey stays the course. If, however, this enabler gets loud or greedy or resorts to revenge or blackmail, they are of no further use. The narcissist wastes no time in devaluing them and cutting all ties. And just like that, the flying monkey disappears.

***

Dear reader, I am again reminding you that I am not qualified to label my ex—or anyone else, for that matter— as a narcissist. To my knowledge, my ex has never been diagnosed as such. The statements contained in this chapter should be interpreted as comparisons between the behavior and characteristics exhibited by my ex with those of the classic narcissist. I will leave my readers to consider these statements and judge for themselves.

6

CONDOMS AND SCHOOL BUSES

My longtime gut feeling that Brian was screwing around was just that, a feeling. I never had proof. Brian was ferociously brilliant at staging events. He covered his tracks without flaw, barely missing a beat.

But that was not always the case. There was a time that he wasn't so careful. In fact, there was actually a day that he got downright sloppy. The kids were still young then. Brian came in at four or five in the morning and shuffled off to sleep on the couch in the rec room, near Greg's bedroom. When I woke up, I went to his room to find out where he had been that night.

I do not remember what he told me, but I'm sure it was a lie. When I got up to leave, something made me turn on the light. That is when I noticed something on the floor in front of Greg's door, something that only Brian could have dropped: a condom, and a used one at that.

Busted, a contrite husband might have said. *You got me* this *time*. Not Brian. It really was quite simple, he said, and a bit funny. He launched into an elaborate, drawn-out tale that came down to this: while he and his buddies were at a strip joint, they went through certain motions only so that they could exact from a stripper the information they needed about party plans. *Nothing more, nothing less,* he added, and *not a topic we need to revisit.* "No big deal, Kathy. It was just a blow job!" *Bullshit.*

Less seedy but equally outlandish was the night I was teaching and Brian was having dinner with a friend. He invited me to join them, but I declined. I was wiped out after a full day at the studio and had to begin another round of classes early the next morning. So Brian ordered dinner for me to take home and brought it out to the car when I drove up to the nice Italian restaurant, a favorite of ours. "Brian, please do not drive home yourself," I said, "I can see that you're already hammered."

"Yeah, okay," he said, "I'll get WeDrive."

I was dozing off to sleep but heard when Brian came into the house. There was the unmistakable smell of McDonald's wafting through the hall and right into my bedroom.

The next morning, as I was leaving for work, I noticed that the entire back window of Brian's truck was gone. He obviously had smashed into something. When I got home that day, I asked him how the windshield shattered.

"Oh yeah, I almost forgot to tell you," he said in a tone that couldn't have been more matter-of-fact. "When I was pulling out of the restaurant, I backed into a school bus that was parked nearby." I listened, waiting for, I don't know, maybe some kind of explanation? Perhaps an apology? Nope. Not a chance.

Now, this all happened on the restaurant's property. Brian and the owners were great friends. I was not worried about trouble from them. But I was floored by Brian's nonchalance in relaying the story. Almost forgot to tell me? What kind of person backs into a school bus, shatters their windshield, waltzes over to grab a greasy fix at the McDonald's Drive Thru, and then falls sound asleep at home?

I remember arguing that point for just a bit and then giving up, outmatched by Brian. *What's the big deal, Kathy? It's just a window. Calm down. There you go, overreacting.*

***

Here, again, I must offer this disclaimer: that I am not qualified to diagnose my ex as a narcissist. Nor is that the intention of this chapter. Readers are encouraged to regard my points as comparisons between my ex's behavior and actions and those of traditional narcissists and to then make their own conclusions.

***

Narcissists are spin doctors. They can deftly push gaslighting to its more extravagant levels. Relying on the old "you're crazy" or "you're overreacting" expressions, they are going beyond the point of causing confusion. They are now making partners doubt their own sanity. Victims not only question their memories, they begin to question their perception of reality. Some begin to question themselves. Some start to feel "crazy."

The roots of this extreme form of gaslighting can be found in the narcissist's identity. Remember, the narcissist has created a public persona very much at odds with what is brewing within. Their exterior is manufactured out of lies and denial. It is built on a mountain of myth. There is the truth and then there is the narcissist's version of what happened. Needless to say, these two accounts are perpetually at odds.

Where does this leave the wife of a narcissist who is reaching the end of her rope? She is dangling in what psychologists refer to as *opposite land*, where the truth is relative and delusion abounds. "Black is white, good is bad, false is true," is how one expert on narcissism has described it. The term is *cognitive dissonance*. It is characterized by inconsistent thoughts, beliefs, and attitudes. It can result from forced behavior, years of compliance and submission, most often to patterns of behavior and ways of thinking that are completely foreign to the victim's own beliefs. It is the psychological equivalent of a nuclear bomb. It crushes the victim's sense of reality and cripples them with uncertainty and fear as if they are staring into the dark abyss, beholding another face of evil.

7

SHOPPING WAS MY DRINK

Will I Ever Be Good Enough? is the title of a best-selling book by a victim of narcissism. I remember coming across that title and wondering what a victim's self-image had to do with narcissism. Boy, was I in for an awakening.

The book is about women raised by narcissistic mothers who pounce on their child's every mistake or shortcoming. The result—sometimes unintended—is to create self-doubt.

It is a method that anyone can use in any setting. It works equally well in a marriage between a narcissistic husband and his unsuspecting wife.

Looking back, it is exactly what happened to me.

Starting at the beginning of our relationship, Brian began chipping away at my self-confidence. He would make jibes about my appearance, take little digs at my abilities. These were not outright insults. He did not intend to engage me in battle. They were more like passing remarks, veiled jabs, the kind of passive-aggressive put down that makes you think twice, lingers in your mind.

"You would look really great in that bathing suit if you lost five pounds," was one remark that comes to my mind. There were others, too. Like the song from the rock band the Presidents of the United States that Brian sang with the kids, "she's lump, she's lump, she's lump," they sang, with Brian changing the next lyric line from "she might be dead" to "she might be *fat*" and, of course, this was always sung within my earshot. Another song he liked to sing with them was by The Monks, "Nice Legs Shame About Her Face." It was hurtful that Brian taught my children to sing these songs and to laugh, as though it wasn't directed at me.

The remarks were scattered and sometimes ambiguous. But each one concealed a deeper meaning. And whether or not I was conscious of it at the time the remarks were made, I realize now that Brian was implying I wasn't so great. It was psychological abuse. He intended it to demoralize me, and it did.

I started to fret about my appearance. I felt not that great about myself. And yes, I started to wonder, *am I good enough?*

I needed a way to cope and found it in a favorite pastime: shopping. I always loved to shop, but I never had the *compulsion* to buy until Brian came into my life. Shopping made me happy, told me I had value. Buying that skimpy black dress made me feel great about myself. Spending a boatload of money made me feel amazing and confident. Shopping was my way of counteracting my husband's outspoken disapproval. It was my dopamine fix.

There was just one problem. My shopping got out of hand. I spent hundreds of thousands of dollars, and I knew it was wrong but . . . I just could not stop.

Until Brian found out. I had gone to great lengths to hide it from him, but I guess I always knew it was just a matter of time before the truth would appear. Money was never a problem in our family. For all his personal flaws, Brian was a wizard at business. He built a thriving company and ran it as tight as a ship. When my credit card purchases caught up with me, Brian took over the finances and bailed me out. Financially, at least, we were on solid ground.

I felt safe again until he made moves that, knowing Brian, I should have expected. He started to throw the whole damn thing in my face. He humiliated me by telling everyone we knew, family, friends, acquaintances, that I ran up huge debt. Instead of covering my mistake, he used it to extract revenge for all the times I had caught him in lies and half-truths.

And he used my shopping compulsion as an excuse for his own bad behavior. Brian was thrilled to finally have something on me. This was too beautiful an opportunity to overlook. Shortly after my mounting bills came to light, Brian booked a guy's trip to South Miami. Rumors of hot body contests and strip joints got back to me.

He didn't have to do that. No one had to know. He could have hidden my flaw from the outside world just as I hid every one of his. I'm talking about all those excuses I made to our kids when Brian missed their events, all those morning phone calls to his company. "Brian is sick and won't be in today." I would make that call every time he blew in from carousing all night, higher than a kite. I did that because I loved him and did not want people to think poorly of him. When you love someone, you keep their secrets, hide their flaws, not drag their name through debris.

Thing is, few people we knew saw the debris that Brian was dragging me through. He figured out that bad-mouthing me was not going to make him look like an angel. So, more often than not, Brian sung my praises and did so behind my back. "Kathy, you don't know what you're talking about! Brian is crazy about you." I heard that so often and from so many people that it makes my head spin just to remember it. "He talks about you constantly," they would say, "he is so proud to have you as his wife."

I know now that it was all a set-up, calculated, and planned by Brian. He played the role of supportive and caring husband to a wife so out there in her thinking that she teetered on the edge of paranoia.

And was it not just like Brian to seize upon my error and blow it out of proportion? He knew what he was doing. He knew I was petrified. We owned a thriving business in St. Catharines. Every important and semi-important person in that city put Brian on a pedestal, and he soaked it all up. His ego swelled. Lawyers, accountants, bankers were in his back pocket, and I was backed into a corner. At any moment, Brian could call on any one of them to do his bidding against me.

I was trapped, overcome by fear. *If people found out about my shopping compulsion, what would happen to me? Where would I end up? Would they take away my beautiful children, more precious to me than anything or anyone?*

Brian could smell my fear. He knew I worried that a fallout between us could have me walking away with nothing, not a dime to my name, not even the respect of my kids. I did not put anything past him, so I clammed up.

I stayed that way for a very long time, and it hurt like hell. But through this whole messy episode, there came a glimmer of light. The boulder that had been my shopping addiction was now removed from my shoulder. I could once again speak my mind without fear of reprisal. There was no longer a secret shame to hide. It was out there, exposed, and for the first time in years, I had a voice. I was free.

The muzzle was off. Now I could get boisterous, rag on Brian without restraint for his extramarital escapades.

What did I have to lose? What's he gonna do now, leave me? *Bring it on!*

***

It came out, several years after these events, that Brian saw a lawyer to discuss our finances because of the shopping excess. Shockingly, Brian considered charging me for the amounts. However, he was restricted by the statute of limitations and was counseled by the lawyer that he was not able to do that. Several more years passed before May 1, 2015, when Brian and I would separate our finances. I did that because I had seen the writing on the wall. I could sense the direction in which the marriage was headed. Today, we are in the middle of divorce proceedings. The irony of it all is that—unbelievably—I will have to sign over most of the equity in the matrimonial home. That is due solely to the bad judgments and investments that Brian made. Canadian family law does not protect the abused, I am sorry to say.

I am now attempting to return us to the status created by the original May 1, 2015 agreement, which was prepared by our accountant. It was an agreement to which both of us pledged to remain faithful, abiding by its terms. However, now that we are pursuing divorce, Brian is pushing for a fifty-fifty split of everything. We did not seek independent legal advice. Funny thing is, Brain was the businessman in our relationship. He should not have even required the independent legal advice that now, quite ironically, he is demanding. So here we are. I will be the one to sign over my portion of the matrimonial home as he continues to push for a fifty-fifty split, even though he—*not I*—is the one who made those poor financial choices.

***

Reader, please remember that I do not intend to diagnose my ex as a narcissist. I am not qualified to make that judgement about him or anyone else. I would merely like to point out the similarities between his behavior and those of narcissists. I leave the judgement-making to you.

Narcissists set unreasonably high standards for their partners and do so with the ulterior motive of making their partners feel inadequate. "Look at me. I'm better than you!" That is the narcissist's message to the world. He channels that into every relationship, whether at work or at home. When he brings that message into his marriage, he does so to cover his lack of genuine self-esteem and his fragile inner man.

This is all part of the narcissist's larger plan. Once the partner is hooked and invested in the relationship, the narcissist begins a steady process of devaluing them. The partner, willing to please, remains on square one. They are always "almost there," close but still very far. They are perpetually stuck on "Go."

The partner's shortcomings are transformed into weaknesses. The narcissist dwells on these as a means of feeding his fragile ego. These people are devoid of a robust self-image. But they make up for that by having the upper hand in every situation. They must always be right. They will win at any cost. They do not stop until a victim is on her knees.

Often, the narcissist brings others into the scheme, although they are not willing participants and usually are clueless about his purpose. No matter. They are not his targets. He has no regard for what others may think about his victim. He is only using others in his attempt to bring down his victim's world, make her believe she is surrounded by people who think her a failure.

Humiliated, the woman retreats into a corner. She may consider herself to be an outcast. She might begin to distance herself from friends and family. That is also part of the plan. "If a man can separate his wife from her family, from everyone she had been close to, then he has accomplished his goal of establishing total control over her," notes a best-selling author on the subject.

Once his wife's shortcomings are labelled as weaknesses, the narcissist begins to exaggerate them. The goal is to manipulate partners into submission. This is most effective when done over time and in spurts. Tiny jabs and pokes, all seemingly innocuous, each reeking of ambiguity.

The jabs and pokes are messages that partners unknowingly internalize. They have adopted the narcissist's opinions of themselves. The mirror shows them what the narcissist has been pointing out all along. A few extra pounds. A sag at the jaw. That squint of indecision. The efforts, however small, send a message: you have not made the grade, you are not good enough, not yet, not ever.

8

OPENING MY BUSINESS AND MY MIND

A cheerleader for the Dallas Cowboys.

That is what I told people I wanted to be when I grew up. It was my dream all through childhood and all those years that I twirled a baton and marched in parades.

And when my dream came true, and I finally made it to the big leagues, I walked away from it.

"Thank you, but no thank you," I told the Hamilton Tiger Cheerleading judges a week after I wowed them with an audition and they invited me to join the squad. "Work and kids," I said, "I am just too busy."

But nothing was further from the truth.

"Really?" Brian said when he learned that I had made the team. "You mean other guys are gonna look at you? Geez. I'm not sure I like that." It was a far cry from what he told his friends. To them, he bragged that his talented wife had the chops to be a professional cheerleader. That's what

Brian said in public. But in private, when no one could hear, he guilted me, and I caved.

He did the same thing years later when I wanted to go back to work. This was when the kids had grown and were busy with teenage life. I had been a stay-at-home mom since Carly was one year old and my employer, the Canada Trust, was downsizing. The bank eliminated middle management, including my position as a loan officer.

By that time, Brian had purchased his own machine shop and was doing exceedingly well. He suggested I stay home and raise the kids full-time. It was a luxury many women would die for. I jumped at the idea and loved every minute of being home with my little ones. But then they grew and needed me less. I still took pride in cooking and cleaning and looking after my family. But being a homemaker no longer fulfilled me.

Ever since childhood, I was the one who felt motivated to do more. I was the teenager who took a job as a bank teller soon after high school graduation and ended up, less than two years later, as a loan officer with the main branch. I had done that through old-fashioned hard work. I took every company-sponsored course I could get my hands on. It paid off big-time until market forces in 1993 beyond my control eliminated my job.

Even then, I needed a diversion, and I found it in physical fitness. It started at age seventeen. I worked part-time as a receptionist for Grantham Fitness Center. I will never forget the first time I walked into that club. People were getting healthy and strong. They were beaming with mental toughness and focus. There was energy. I was wowed. That is where it started, my love of fitness. That was my calling.

I told the manager that it was my dream to teach one of his fitness classes. He sensed my enthusiasm and took me under his wing. With his guidance, I took class after class: CanFitPro, personal training, group fitness, cycling, muscle, and nutrition decision. Through the years I was able to accumulate thirteen certificates.

Once I was certified, I auditioned for a teaching position and passed. Now I was in my element. I no longer did reception. I had my own classes, my own students, and a passion all my own.

I loved it so much that even with a full-time day job at the bank, I couldn't give up my teaching side gig. Then motherhood found me, and there was no longer any time to teach. But I still managed to stay on top of my craft. I went to fitness exhibits in Toronto, took group spinning classes, worked out regularly in my home gym. All the while, I knew that fitness was in my bones. And someday, as soon as I'd get the chance, I would go back to it.

The chance came in the early 2000s. I completed CORE certification, an intense four days of written examinations, auditions, and nine hours on the bike. That got me a job teaching one spin class at The Revolution Gym. The owners liked me so much, they asked me to teach six more classes.

My confidence soared. I was building my own circle of friends and making the right business connections. I was feeding my years-long urge to be productive. The Kathy who somehow got lost in the four walls of her home had sprung back to life. There was no way to contain my enthusiasm. I imagined taking my ambition to the next level and opening my own fitness club. And while I was on top of the world, spreading my wings, Brian was having none of it. He started to seethe.

"It'll screw up the taxes if you start a business," he said. But he wasn't fooling me. His excuse for not wanting me to have my own club had nothing to do with taxes and everything to do with his ego. The bigger my following of fitness clients, the more sought-after my teaching became, the more jealous Brian was becoming. He did not like taking a back seat to my career. He hated that I couldn't stay out late at social events with him because I was teaching a class at six o'clock the next morning. Even worse, I was out and about, not contained in the house, climbing out from under Brian's thumb.

"Okay, you go on home. I'll stay out." He started to say those things to me on our occasional date-nights out. Over time, those occasional nights became more frequent. Brian started going out without me. We were drifting apart. Things went from bad to worse pretty darn fast.

But that was before my job at The Revolution Gym. Things were different for me then. I had found my niche. I was shaking the doubts. I was ready to stand up to Brian's standby excuse—"It'll screw up the taxes"—which had long kept me from getting a job. It wasn't going to work anymore. The cocoon had burst. There wasn't a damn thing that Brian could do to stop me.

"I don't care about the taxes," I said. "I'm going to open a gym." I went ahead and began looking for vacant retail space. When Brian saw that his resistance was not making me back down, he gave up and did an abrupt about-face. All of a sudden, my running a business was a grand idea. He helped me to find the right building and negotiate a purchase.

I now see his change of heart as yet another power play. He figured out there was no way to stop me. So he might as well come along for the ride. We had the money. I was determined to do it. Rather than have it appear that his wife opened a business without his approval, he would much rather be the supportive husband who was permitting me to branch out. And let's not forget how a full-time job for me would make playtime simpler for Brian. That was 2013, and Climaxx Cycling was born. Conceived, branded, and run by me.

Opening day was August 9, 2014. It was exhilarating and daunting at the same time. I was all too aware that fitness in St. Catharines was a mighty competitive field. As a start-up, I would have to establish myself, gain people's trust, keep prices low enough to build a customer base. It was true of most new businesses. They struggle through the first few years. Climaxx Cycling did, too. Sales were lower than I expected, and Brian used my lack of profits to pick fights.

One night he came home drunk, and we got into a kerfuffle. Brian erupted with such venom that I was expecting at any moment the fight would turn physical. He became aggressive, ranting like a maniac, demanding that I leave the house at once and not wait until the morning, as I had suggested. He called my parents at 3 a.m. "Come and get her right this minute," he said, "I hate her guts!" My parents ran to help me, and when Brian called me a "piece of shit," my father couldn't remain an impartial bystander. He stepped closer to Brian, who had now become more confrontational, screaming all kinds of obscenities, calling me names and letting the word "loser" spill out of his mouth.

Days later, the fight and that word came up in conversation. "That's very hurtful!" I said.

"Well, you made me mad!" He did everything but cross his arms and stomp his feet.

That blow-up was another example of Brian's lack of emotional support during Climaxx's critical first years. It was a giant letdown, though not really a surprise. The business opening was a reminder to Brian that his negativity was losing its sway over me.

I pressed on. I navigated the learning curves and made great friends along the way. Throwing myself into a business deferred a lot of my mental chaos. It gave me something besides a rocky marriage to absorb. In return, I learned that I am magnificent and worthy and have tremendous value in this world.

Above all, it was a turning point. Years ago, Brian's menacing words caused me to walk away from cheerleading, my lifelong goal. In the name of love I had already given up one dream. There was no way in hell that I was going to let this new one pass me by.

***

Herewith is my usual disclaimer: I am not certified to make a diagnosis that my ex is or ever was a narcissist. Only a professional can do that. My statements in this and every other chapter are to be construed merely as comparisons between my ex's behavior and those of most narcissists. Readers are encouraged to consider my descriptions and to form their own opinions.

***

The only way for a narcissist to thrive in a family setting is for family life to revolve around their needs. That requires a partner willing to submit and go the distance.

Nothing is more unsettling to the narcissist than to see their partner showing signs of independence, either of thought or action. Before entering the relationship, the narcissist goes to extreme lengths to select partners who by nature acquiesce to their goals. Even more time is spent on conditioning the partner to back down at every turn. The slightest pushback from the partner is all it takes for the narcissist to believe he is going to be betrayed. His retaliation is swift, and the partner falls back in line, bending around the narcissist's needs.

But then the moment comes. An idea. A flash of insight. The partner remembers an old itch. They develop a fire in the belly. It gets vocalized, and the narcissist's antenna shoots up. They smell a threat.

It is not a question of whether but how the narcissist will react. Open or passive aggression. It does not matter. Both work just fine. It can start with the narcissist contrasting a partner's mediocre results with his own grandiose accomplishments. "It's great that you have made the track team after all these years of trying. But before I was even out of high school, I was winning marathons." That "compliment" is typical of the passive-aggressive reaction the narcissist doles out to dampen a partner's enthusiasm. The two-fold purpose is to feed the narcissist's ego and to prevent the partner from believing she has what it takes to go further. She must not be allowed to develop her sense of self. She should never find her worth.

9

EPIPHANY

f I can't beat him, I'll join him.

That sums up my mentality in 2013. Brian was still carrying on, and I was still waiting for him to wake up and see that his horseplay was ripping us apart. Clearly when it came to partying like the world would not end, Brian was ahead of me. The only thing I could do was to join him. I reconciled myself to becoming the wife who learns to shoot a gun so she can join her husband at the range. Maybe going out together was a way for us to stay close, I thought. Maybe we could reclaim the deep connection that I thought we once had. Maybe Brian would even want to change for me, for us.

It was a long shot. Partying was never my thing. But I was going to give it my all, ride it as long as I could. I pulled it off for a good six months until I looked in the mirror and did not see me.

I opened my heart to Brian. I could no longer play the role of party animal. "You're leaving me no choice but to cheat on you," he said, a response that I should have seen coming and probably did, a response that, by the way, I brought up on several occasions thereafter only to hear his default excuse: "Oh, I was just kidding!"

What to do next I had not one clue. I could not see many options. So I did what I had done for years. I hoped and prayed and stayed in the marriage until I couldn't anymore.

Breaking point number one came on New Year's Day 2014. Brian, the kids, and I had been to a New Year's Eve party. The kids and I were ready to leave, but Brian wanted to stay. "Your family is here, your son is home from college," I said, "do you really have to party after 1:00 a.m.?"

He did, he said. He was having fun and wanted to stay a little longer.

So we left without him, not knowing that "a little longer" to us did not have the same meaning that it had for Brian.

Nine o'clock the next morning, Carly, her husband, and I were having coffee at the kitchen table. In walked Brian, wearing the same suit from the night before, looking very strung out. I could feel my heart pounding against my chest. My forehead tightened. I felt pressure in the back of my head.

I let hours go by, allowed Brian to catch up on sleep, and then I confronted him.

"I'm done," I said. "I want you out."

"You knew where I was," he said.

"That makes it alright?"

The next thing I knew, Brian had brought the kids

together in the living room. We all were going "to talk." "Mom's throwing me out," he said. Carly—who had been right there when he stumbled in just hours ago—burst into tears. Greg was in shock.

Nice going, Brian, I wanted to say, once again, this is all on me. Though I have since forgotten all the words tossed around in that room that day, I had the feeling that Brian was victorious at manipulating our kids' emotions.

He then made arrangements to move. I was still looking for another way out. "Brian, listen to me. We can work on this, but you need to promise me you'll get help."

He bristled at the idea. "Oh, that wouldn't look good," he said. "I have already told people I'm moving out."

So what, then, was the reason for his little charade with the kids just hours before? It took time, but I now see that Brian considered my asking him to move out a once-in-a-lifetime chance for more shenanigans. He would shack up with single buddy, Mike and spend a month or two living the bachelor's life. Mike handed Brian a set of house keys. Brian could come and go as he pleased, just as he did at our house, on the excuse of using the gym downstairs. The frequent pop-ins gave Brian an open window to my activities while I—who did not have keys to Mike's house—had no idea what Brian was doing behind my back.

The set-up was unbelievably convenient for Brian. Working out at the home gym gave him the chance to run into me frequently, and that is what did us in. I was still his wife. I still wanted to be the only woman to satisfy his physical needs.

The separation ended up with Brian having the best of both worlds. At Mike's, he was free to let loose. And at home, he had a warm bed and a wife who had no intention of driving him into another woman's arms. All of my admonishing about the purpose of our separation fell on deaf ears. "This is not free time for you to go around and screw whomever you want," I had made it clear to Brian right from the start. The point was for him to reflect on his behavior, on our marriage. To understand that he needed help.

"If you need to use this separation to be with other women, we are done," I said. "Understand?"

"I do," Brian said. But he did not, and it wasn't too long before Brian was packing his things to move back home. Days later, we were at Carly's house for Sunday dinner. Carly was scrolling through Brian's cell. She stopped at a picture of a woman she didn't recognize. "Mom, it was a selfie," she said much later, "and the girl looked like a stripper." In time, the goings-on at Mike's house and the girl Mike was dating came up in conversation between me and Brian. He was buzzed and probably did not even recognize his own wife sitting across from him when he blurted out this little gem: "But I didn't get her pregnant." *Great job, Brian.*

Thinking back to our trial run at separation, I have to admit that having sex with Brian was counterproductive. I wasn't just letting him back into the house. I was allowing him back into my heart. He made love exquisitely, like magic. In a flash, he could take me back to a season of ecstasy and make me want to hold on forever, at least until his next shady move.

The same abusive cycle repeated itself when we next separated in 2016. By that time, I was engrossed in my business and thankful that long work days kept me away from tensions at home. But as hard as I worked, I could not deny the emotional toll that a failing marriage was having on me. My nerves were raw. My mind lacked clarity.

This time, I was the one who moved out, to a townhouse I had purchased earlier as an investment but knew deep down I would end up living in alone. Thus began a year of back and forth, comings and goings, fighting and love bombing, and a little extra wine for comfort at night. But wine and work were short-term comforts. In the long stretch, I missed my husband.

Two separations in two years. What did I learn? That there was no real love from Brian in this relationship. I was the only one in love. And also that I would remain blind to the source of our marital dysfunction until I parceled out the reasons that brought Brian back to my door: he had his fill of fooling around and wanted someone to care for him again. But the pattern dragged on. He was never going to stop professing his love for me, swearing he had done no wrong, just as he was never going to curtail his urge to frolic.

I am pretty sure that I saw this more clearly soon after the 2014 separation. It was one of those "What just happened?" moments. I sorted through the events in my mind, the mismatch between Brian's actions and his words, and concluded that it was futile for us to keep doing the same thing but expecting different results.

And there it was, my epiphany.

***

Reader, before I move on with my research findings, I will remind you that I am not a medical professional, and I am thoroughly unqualified to make a diagnosis of narcissism in regard either to my ex or to any other individual. Please remember that my statements are mere suggestions that my ex's behavior was strikingly similar to that of the classic narcissist. I will not make any opinions on the matter. I leave that to you.

***

It is called *divide and conquer,* a strategy used by narcissists to seize control of the situation at hand, especially one that concerns their family. They create divisions among individuals, most often the children the couple share. The children are the group that is divided and thus weakened. Once they become pawns in the narcissist's scheme, they are vulnerable to all sorts of manipulation.

This fractured family becomes an ideal platform for the narcissist to present himself as the victim. He will turn the tables on his wife, the real victim, but also the de facto target of his abuse.

Divide and conquer is a strategy often used when there is the threat of exposure, such as a physical separation for a marriage. The wife may see the separation as a time-out, a restorative break. In her well-intentioned mind, they are not breaking up, they are merely taking a break. The point is for the narcissist to reflect on his behavior and hopefully to seek help.

But that rarely happens. The narcissist rarely believes he needs help. There is no effort to change his behavior unless it is in his own interest to do so. His wife's grievances do not hold enough sway.

Few partners ever realize this. They seek a variety of ways to rehabilitate the narcissist. But that mindset presupposes the narcissist has genuine love for the partner and is fully invested in the relationship, which is often not the case. It also presumes the narcissist has the capacity for objective reflection—to remove himself from the situation and see how his behavior contributed to the relationship's demise.

That is a fairy tale.

One of the most shocking realizations for victims of narcissistic marriages is to find out they were in love alone. There was never real emotional buy-in. The narcissist never saw the partner for who she is. The victim is the object to be manipulated for the narcissist's own goals.

10

TRIGGERED

t was Thanksgiving weekend 2019. I called Greg at the University of Victoria.

"Want me to come up and make you a nice Thanksgiving dinner?"

Greg rarely had the chance to come home between semesters.

"Wow, that would be so great!" he said.

Brian thought so too. We set a date and bought the tickets to spend the holiday with our son.

As departure day approached, Brian had a change of plans. His friend's daughter was getting married that weekend, and he just had to go. I had known about the wedding too. The bride was the daughter of a friend we barely saw.

"Really?" I said. "So you'd prefer to go to the wedding of a girl you hardly know rather than spend a holiday weekend with your son, whom you get to see maybe twice a year?"

"I want to support Sal," Brian said. "This will give you and Greg alone time, like I had with him when I went last year."

Brian said he would join us in BC that Sunday after the wedding. It has always been a challenge for me to say no to Brian, so I gave in, overlooking the fact that Brian's new plan made no sense. Round trip to Victoria costs $1,500. Why spend that much money for two days in BC instead of five?

Thursday came, I flew to Victoria. Brian had once again finagled a nice stretch of days when he was home alone, and I was five thousand miles away. The next day, Brian called me and announced his big new plans for that night. He was splurging on a dinner for my parents, his mom, and his sister. It sounded like a big ordeal. I hung up the phone asking myself why? Why did Brian suddenly feel the need to celebrate the holiday with relatives? What would make him go through all that trouble when I wasn't there to help?

As Friday wore on, Brian's behavior raised even more questions. He went out of his way to check in with me and Carly. The man who had no trouble disappearing from home for hours, even days, suddenly could not relax until his wife and daughter knew where he would be, and what he would be doing that night. And to think, neither of us had bothered to ask.

Turns out, Brian was cooking more than just dinner that night. But I did not have an inkling of that until Saturday morning when I dialed Brian's number at seven o'clock, the time he should have been up, and got no answer. So I texted him. No reply. I called a second and third time. Still no answer, until I sent this text: "Are you fucking kidding me?"

Suddenly, the phone rang. Brian sounded like he hadn't slept in years.

"Every single time that I'm away," I said, "this is how you behave?"

It reminded me of the month before, when I was in New York City. It was around 9 or 10 p.m. when Brian texted me. "I'm at the shop, getting work done. I will be here for a few more hours, and then I'll head home. Love you!" In other words, "I am texting you now so you won't bother me later."

The next morning, I texted him at 7:00 a.m. his time because I knew he should have been up by then. There was no reply. So I texted him at 7:30 a.m. and again at 8:00 a.m. and again at 8:30 a.m. I received no replies to any of these texts. At this point, I knew he was up to no good. So I phoned him at 9:00 a.m., and my suspicions were correct

That is how things went in New York, and clearly that was what he was doing now.

"Who is in my fucking house?!!" I demanded.

He got defensive. "Kath," he said, "there's nobody here!"

The events of the last two days raced through my mind. Brian had orchestrated the Friday night dinner party to stop my mom and dad from showing up unannounced, which they sometimes did. They had their own key. Mom had mentioned stopping by that weekend to say hello and drop things off in the garage. My gut told me that Brian's dinner party on Friday night was his way of getting family out of the way so no one would bother him later.

Yup, I thought , *after the dinner party for the family, Brian had his own little party.*

I hung up and ignored him. I sat quietly for a few minutes and let thoughts flood in. *Kathy, you've been doing this for far too many years. When are you going to learn?*

By Sunday, Brian was shooting off text messages as if our clash on Saturday never happened. "Everything's good!" He showed up at Greg's place and said, "Give me a kiss."

My concern was Greg. I did not want him to feel uncomfortable. I remembered Mom telling me what Greg had told her in confidence, what made my stomach ill. He was happy living away at college. He could not take the yelling and screaming at home.

Brian put his things down and got comfortable. Minutes later, he was deep into this over-the-top story about his post-dinner activities on Friday night. Apparently he spilled chips on the bed and did not have time to clean the mess. He spared no detail in telling us how he had eaten chips in bed but had then fallen asleep, only to wake and find that there was no time to clean the mess. He had an early flight to catch and had to rush out of the house. His story was much too elaborate. I felt that Brian was setting me up for something, and that feeling only intensified after I had found out—from two separate people—that while Brian did in fact go to Sal's daughter's wedding, he stayed for only two hours and left right after dessert.

On the way home to St. Catharines on Tuesday, Brian would not let go of the messy chips story. "Don't forget we have to change the sheets!" he said during the drive home. He shook his head. "I still can't believe I fell asleep with those chips right next to me!"

We got home. We changed the sheets. I could not hold back.

"If I told anyone the trouble you went through to have me out of the house just so you could have Saturday all to yourself, people would think I'm crazy," I said. "But then again, Brian, isn't that the point?"

He laughed.

***

Three days of silence followed our return from BC.

Brian caved first. "So we need to talk about this," he said.

"Right now, Brian, there is nothing to talk about. I want a divorce."

There, I said it. The "d" word. Brian's mood went from zero to 3,000. "Well, we're gonna tell everybody that we're getting a divorce!"

Christmas was right around the corner. Greg's midterms were coming up.

"Fine," I said, "we can tell everyone we're divorcing, but we should wait until after Greg's exams."

"Nope," he said, "we're doing it right now!"

Although I was the one who asked for a divorce, Brian had to be the one to tell people. It was his way of stealing my thunder, taking control.

He picked up the phone and called Greg the night before a big exam.

"I am so sorry, Greg," I said afterward. "I begged Dad not to say anything until after your test."

"No problem, Mom," said Greg, who ended up passing anyway.

Greg was coming home for Christmas break. I planned to stay in the house with him through Christmas and move out in January. But staying for just a few more weeks was a struggle, so I moved out earlier. Brian slept by day, partied all night, and continued to arrive home at four in the morning. The pattern reminded me of all the turmoil I had lived through and why, after what seemed like centuries, I was finally pulling the plug.

***

Before presenting my research results on the events of this chapter, I would like to remind the reader that I am not qualified to diagnose my ex or anyone else as a narcissist. However, my ex displayed characteristics and behaviors that are normally associated with narcissistic personalities. I am merely pointing out those similarities. I will not make any conclusions on the diagnosis. I leave that entirely to the reader.

***

More often than not, the partners of a narcissist are unwilling to see the relationship for what it is. They linger well beyond the point at which they should have been gone. They have been on the receiving end of abuse for far too long. But uncertainty lurks in their mind, largely the product of the narcissist's doing: *You are a loser. You will never amount to more than you are now. No one will ever love you. You will never find one as good as me.*

Thus, the partner avoids having to make the ultimate decision: *Do I stay or do I leave?* Though most have convinced their minds that the only rational choice is to leave, their hearts are usually not in sync.

They spend years, even decades, hoping for a change, subsisting on the sparse moments that the narcissist shows their good side. It is at this point that partners decide they can bear the trauma for not one day longer. Their sense of self is nearly demolished. Their emotions and self-esteem have withered. They begin to reflect deeply. *What have I become? What am I doing, and why?* If the partner can separate the man from his actions and focus on the abuse, they can see that the list of reasons to leave far exceeds the list of reasons to stay. The only rational decision is to break free.

A partner's decision to leave the relationship comes as a severe blow to the narcissist's ego. They perceive that their meticulously choreographed world is crumbling. They fear exposure. Could they possibly be losing a battle? These thoughts unnerve them and make them lash out, causing *narcissistic injury*, which can have devastating repercussions for the victim.

The choice of divorce shifts focus away from the narcissist's misstep that caused the divorce and centers focus on the partner's decision to leave. The partner, who is the real victim, is now portrayed by the narcissist as the aggressor. She is ungrateful for all those years that he provided support, and now she is seeking to destroy a happy home and the excellent husband who made it all possible.

The threat of divorce also causes narcissists to put on airs. He cannot show that he has been injured because, in his mind, injury gives off the signal that he is weak. So the narcissist cops an attitude. The divorce is a mere disturbance in his life, a foolish skirmish, something that does not even rise to the level of annoyance in him. But deep down, he is boiling. At this point, his aggression may become open. To hell with the victims; he has no regard for who gets hurt.

11

CUTTING THE TIES

Well, I did it. I emptied my nest and prepared to spread my wings. Brian was in the past, and the past was now history. It was 2020. New year, new woman.

And more important was my new way of life. There would be no more back and forth with Brian, no more games. He was now free to pursue his whims wherever they might take him. I was flying solo, not entirely sure of my direction but prepared nevertheless for things to go sideways, at least in the beginning.

Of course, they did. But the tight spots came mostly in spurts, tiny moments that happen throughout any day. At night, I will admit, there was some loneliness, and discomfort too. I did think of going back to Brian. I did use wine, one glass, sometimes three, to push those moments away. I was at a particularly low point when along came a friend, a very good soul, who dropped one line and, just like that, put it all into perspective: "What is this great thing you're getting from Brian that you think you can't give to yourself?"

Stop. Reflect. Reboot. I put down the wine and started coping with my newfound liberation the best way I knew how. I resumed my vigorous workouts. I now had time to get deeper into meditation, one of those interests that caught my attention but for which I could never find the time.

I even started a private journal. This was much more than a record of what happened. My writing was not merely a rehash of my relationship in storybook form. I needed to process my feelings, and journaling helped me sort through the confusion, anger, and blur. It became a magical restorative. Once I started to write, I could not stop. I think I filled five solid notebooks. The pain really was that sharp. This time, I would make sure the journal did not "disappear," as every journal—and my passport—had in the past disappeared when I was living in the same house as Brian.

A week or two into that regimen, and I was recharged. Just in time to endure more go-arounds with Brian, who was now pulling out all the stops to wear me down. By then I had been conditioned to the love bombing, so much so that the interval between Brian showing his good and bad sides had shortened considerably.

The mixed signals from him started almost immediately. When I first moved out, Brian pretended not to notice. But he soon went back to wooing me. Once, during a snowstorm on a Sunday when we were expected for dinner at Carly's, he called to offer me a lift. "I know you don't like to drive in the snow," Brian said, "how about I pick you up and drive you there?" *No, thank you.*

Next came a dinner invitation "to talk."

"Kathy, you know we're not getting a divorce," Brian said after a few sips of wine. I brought up him announcing our divorce to Greg, him kicking aside my concerns. I told him I had figured out his little scheme, that he had agreed to separate just to buy a month of freedom until that got old, and he would come crawling back to me.

"You said you were moving into your condo," he said.

"No, I didn't," I said, "but that's a nice twisting of my words." The conversation went downhill from there, and I got up to leave.

The invitations kept coming. I often gave in. Brian sounded genuine, and I needed to know I had the inner strength to face Brian, tell him nothing had changed, I was still out. But every time we met, I felt as though I were walking into a lion's den. I would psyche myself up, get there feeling strong, and say what I wanted to say only to have Brian talk circles around my words. When I resisted, he began the familiar tirade: "That's it! We're done! I'm calling my lawyer!" Go right ahead, I would reply. Time went by— an hour, sometimes two days—and he backpedaled around to square one.

I fared better when we met in public. When Brian got loud, it was easy to get up and walk out. That was much harder to do when the dinners were at home. In that cozy and familiar setting, I would walk in to wine glasses on the table, music playing in the background, family pictures on the walls, and the smell of a gourmet meal Brian was cooking for just us two. The mood became hypnotic. I was travelling back in time to romance, and to the man I had cherished for years.

So I learned to stand my guard, be ready for the next smoke screen. It happened in mid-December 2019 when Brian announced—again—that he did not want a divorce. To avoid drama around the holidays, I told him we would address it later. We focused on the kids. We rented a limousine to take us all into Toronto for a nice dinner and a play. But things turned sour when Brian kept hitting the bottle. In the time it took my son-in-law, Norm, and I to have one glass of wine, Brian had downed two along with four beers. He started to get arrogant and to spout off some stupid stuff. I asked him to stop. I might have used the word "pretender."

All hell broke loose. Something about that word touched a nerve in him. Brian made a scene. He got up and stormed out of the restaurant, hailing a cab, and riding by himself the two hours back to St. Catharines. None of us were surprised. We had been through this with him before. We finished dinner and headed home. During the ride, we received a barrage of angry texts from Brian: "I hate you so much!" (to me) and "The marriage is over! I am done for good!" (to the kids).

But that was December. Come January, he was singing my praises, back to schmoozing again.

***

Reader, I am not certified to diagnose my ex as a narcissist. That is not my intention in this or any other chapter of the book. Please construe my statements and descriptions as comparisons between his behavior and actions and those of typical narcissists. I refrain from making any conclusions on such a diagnosis.

***

Narcissists make those around them unhappy. Often, it is not a question of if but when a partner will tire of the abusive patterns, the mayhem, and take flight.

With the partner gone or threatening to leave, there is no one for the narcissist to control. They feel powerless. By instinct, they attempt to bring the partner back into their orbit of command. It is a process the experts call *hoovering*, which refers to a vacuum sucking action. Promising to change and dangling gifts are two of the most common ways a narcissist hoovers, trying to reel in their longtime victim.

When a partner asks for a divorce, focus shifts away from the narcissist's grand accomplishments to their misdeeds. They now feel backed into a corner. But they can twist the situation by baiting their partners into arguments. The narcissist knows how to bring out the worst in their partner. By embroiling them in a useless debate, they can provoke

85

them to anger, and play the victim.

The baited argument also becomes a platform for the narcissist to reestablish their control and superiority. Controversy is the stage on which these personalities perform best. They shine under a spotlight of strife. The partner strikes back, the narcissist counters, and the same old cycle repeats and drags on.

An invitation "to talk" is so much more than that. It is really a back-handed attempt to lure the victim into an event that sounds productive. But the truth is that the narcissist has no such intention. The invitation is a ruse for a meeting designed to showcase narcissistic cruelty. The narcissist will engage the victim in mindless arguments. Once baited, the victim flounders in a game they cannot win. The narcissist knows their insecurities. It takes them no time to disable the victim's confidence. In minutes, a victim can be in a daze, wondering "What in the world just happened?"

Other times, instead of arguing, the narcissist will show *faux innocence*. This has the appearance of concern. Many victims are deceived into believing that the narcissist is having a change of heart about their behavior during the relationship. But the whole point of faux innocence is to catch the victim off guard.

The narcissist might begin the meeting by rambling on about everyday topics. The relationship break-up is the elephant in the room that is never addressed. But remember, the narcissist's goal is to ensnare the victim in battle and to do so without their noticing. These people are experts at circular conversation. The victim walks into an argument they never saw coming.

The conversation then shifts. The narcissist's language is ablaze with ad hominem attacks and gaslighting phrases that disarm the victim, now frustrated and confused. Many victims of these contrived scenarios say they left without ever knowing what caused the argument or even what it was about.

One of the reasons that divorce brings out the worst in these people is that the narcissist does not relish taking account of his actions. Divorce is perceived as the end of the line. The partner is saying, "Enough. I'm out." The narcissist feels that their mistakes have caught up with them. This triggers another particularly cruel kind of counter-attack. Looking for ways to funnel his anger, the spurned narcissistic husband takes to digital abuse. He lashes out at his wife in text messages and emails. The tenor of these communications reveals ferocity. The sheer number of them show the narcissist's capacity for unrelenting warfare.

Digital abuse reveals the narcissist's refusal to allow his partner any boundaries. At first, victims see digital communications as a plus. It is a relief they do not have to meet face-to-face and wither under his spell. It is also a benefit during legal proceedings to have written proof of the narcissist's harassing messages.

But there is a dangerous downside to digital

communications: they are easy and accessible at any moment. They provide the narcissist with an open door to his victim any time of day or night. In the dead of night, if the narcissist feels provoked or recalls a grievance, he does not have to get in his car and drive anywhere to confront his victim. Mobile devices and digital communication have made it easy for him to reach over to his cell on the nightstand, unload hair-raising texts, and then roll over back to sleep.

Most narcissists use social media to hook up with new flings in order to make their partners jealous. Brian flat-out refused to use social media. That made perfect sense to me. Players like him are exposed much more quickly and easily and have their infidelities confirmed. In fact, Brian practically admitted this when he told me he used the app "What's App" because it wasn't traceable.

Although Brian did not use social media (and, I suspect, the reason is that he never wanted to be identified by one of his possible one-night stands), I did learn that during one of our separations, he signed up for "fuckbook" and "Instafuck" but no other social media. Right up until the day that I left, Brian was responding to indiscreet and random hookups of which I have proof.

Digital communications are the method of choice for narcissists who feel spurned and are crazed with revenge. They use the entire landscape of social media to inundate their partner and paralyze them with fear. The victim feels surrounded by hostility, even feeling they are being stalked.

They end up dazed and terror-stricken. They have no idea where to turn for relief. "What will he do next?" becomes the question of the day and minute. A truly sadistic twist of fate is that the narcissist has succeeded in becoming his victim's main event. All of her thoughts and energies—temporarily diverted to her new goal of breaking free from him—are rerouted to focus on him.

To cope with the chaos, the partner becomes hypervigilant. Divorced women describe being always on guard so they can anticipate their husband's next move. Some women have described standing in dark rooms and peering through the curtains, expecting him to show up at their doorstep for another round of clashes.

12

WHY DON'T YOU JUST LEAVE?

heard that question so many times. I wanted to say, geez, I wish I'd thought of that! Here is the scientific reason why I couldn't "just leave."

Emotionally and psychologically abusive relationships don't have scars for the outside world to see. Combine that with a "Dr. Jekyll-Mr. Hyde" personality that I alone saw as my ex's true personality.

Emotional abuse destroys your self-esteem, making you feel it's impossible to get a fresh start. I really didn't even realize I was being abused until the marriage was over. There were minimal physical altercations and never any violence. Also, many people downplay emotional abuse because they don't regard it as being as bad as physical abuse. It was very hard for me to leave the relationship. I did try nine or ten times to leave. My ex made me feel worthless, that I had no better option for a companion than him. He would constantly tell me, "You will never find anyone else."

It was only at the end of the marriage that I also realized the *honeymoon phase*—or the phase when my ex appeared to love me—was part of the abusive cycle. Often, the abuse was followed by my ex's attempt to minimize the event. He would buy me something or "do something nice" for me.

It can be very dangerous to leave an emotionally abusive relationship. I've had several conversations with my doctor, which revealed that the more I returned to the abusive relationship, the higher was the chance of me becoming physically abused or a homicide statistic. Now, I'm not saying that would happen. These are just the statistics. The more times a victim returns to an abusive relationship, the more they face the chance of physical violence or worse. I did feel that each time I returned to my home. The honeymoon phase and "niceness" would be shorter and shorter, and the abuse would carry on longer and longer. It was almost like I was being punished because I contemplated leaving. A couple of the earliest times that I packed up and decided to leave, the words, "I will make your kids hate you!" and "I will destroy you!!" were the final words I heard. But those were also the words that brought me back because, quite frankly, my ex scared the shit out of me when he was angry. His eyes would grow twice the size, and it was like there was no soul inside him. I remember thinking, *I have no idea who you are.*

After every single conflict, I was made to feel like everything was my fault. He would turn the situation around and make me feel guilty and would continually gaslight me. One of my ex's famous lines was, "That didn't happen." In fact, the non-stop gaslighting became the reason for me to start keeping a journal. How interesting that five of the six journals I kept at home suspiciously disappeared. As soon as I started keeping them at my studio, they stopped going missing. The journals allowed me to look back at events and to know the truth about them so I didn't believe my ex's version. He was trying to convince me that I was going crazy. I wasn't. He was gaslighting me. One of the last conflicts was with this exact scenario: he blew up when I called him on his tactics and ghosted me for four days. I guess he had plans with another supply and needed justification for bad behavior.

And probably the number one reason that makes leaving an abusive relationship difficult is the *trauma bonding*. As humans, we are hardwired to survive trauma bonds—something often compared to and used interchangeably with Stockholm Syndrome. Trauma bonds start to take shape when someone receives intermittent reinforcement. A good example of intermittent reinforcement in a romantic relationship is that you reach out for support and sometimes your partner offers support, other times not. Often when you ask why you're not receiving the support you need, you're lied to or told in some way that you're not deserving of the support or that the support is conditional or has strings attached. These trauma bonds can't form in a healthy relationship with its absence of abuse. The abuse itself is actually the thing that forms those bonds in the first place, making it feel impossible to leave. Because of the nature of the cycle of abuse—the tension building stage, the incident, reconciliation, and honeymoon phase—there are profound impacts on our bodies and brains. During the incident of abuse, the stress hormone cortisol can be activated in the body. Although cortisol is an important hormone for humans, having large amounts can cause long-term illness. (I will go further into this in the next chapter. After I left the marriage, I was diagnosed with post-traumatic stress disorder.)

While cortisol and its consequences are dire, it's important to note that it's not the only hormone working against abuse victims. During the reconciliation and honeymoon phases, dopamine has a role in making the abuse victim seek comfort at the hands of their abuser. This hormonal roller coaster is addictive to the abuse victim.

The trauma bond means often the abuse victim does not see themselves as a victim or anything particularly wrong with their relationship. Even when they do try to leave, they find that when they get away from their abuser, they will miss their abuser due to the trauma bonding. A trauma bond is what had me trying to fix a man who was breaking me.

That was my problem—I left but I couldn't stay away. Abusers seem to be able to sense vulnerability and often reel their victims back in with empty promises that they will change or things will be better, only for the abuse to continue and, usually, to get worse.

Again, however, I am not labeling my ex as a narcissist. I am thoroughly unqualified to make that determination. I am merely suggesting that his behaviors and actions bear a striking resemblance to those of classic narcissists. Readers are encouraged to make their own judgments.

13

HERE AND NOW

"Let's have dinner." That was Brian's text to me on Valentine's Day 2020.

My knee-jerk reaction was to go. I love romance. But I have felt like a hamster on a wheel for far too long. I cannot keep running in circles. Motion for motion's sake is not going to deliver progress. So I declined. I know Brian is not sincere about showing his emotions, he is just playing on mine. Saying no to him was a first big step in the right direction.

An even bigger step was closing Climaxx Cycling Studio on December 24, 2019. The decision was anything but easy and came after profound contemplation. It had nothing to do with the twisted story Brian spun to family, friends, anyone who would listen, that I was closing my studio and walking away from my clients so I could focus more on him.

The truth is that I did it for my clients. I am rebranding Climaxx from a class-based business into one that caters to individuals with personal training and online events.

There will be the same strong focus on fitness, nutrition, and positive mindset, and a new focus on resilience and empowerment. Everything I have done up to this point has led me to this new business model that will open soon.

There will be a new focus on meditation and resilience mindset. We will make sure that the inner work is done first. It has changed my life and taught me how to change others' lives too. Like the team of twelve who came to me when they were training for an indoor rowing competition and were not sure they could pull it off. I mapped out an individualized training regimen for them, one that added visualization and meditation to their usual Friday night classes. We did that right up until the night before the 2,000 meter race, which they totally crushed. It was a personal win for me too. Their success reaffirmed for me that I have a flair for inspiring the best in others.

An even deeper truth is that I paused Climaxx for *me*. After five years of pouring my sweat into my business, I needed a healthier work-life balance. I had been in this marriage for most of my life, and my life was zooming by. My work, however gratifying, worthy, and self-fulfilling it was, had inhaled me.

I needed to reflect on the past, reconnect with my core values, and find myself. I remember my staff and I shutting down on Christmas Eve. Many of them were crying, but I could not shed a single tear. Was I that detached in spirit from the one undertaking that taught me I had real value?

"You've packed all your emotions so far down that you've lost the ability to feel," said a life coach who knows what he's talking about.

Before I could look to the future, I needed to let go of the past, the bitterness stirred up by my rough-and-tumble marriage, now approaching its third decade. Anger had consumed me. I knew that I needed to forgive Brian so as not to burn with hate.

I turned to meditation, and boy, am I glad that I did. There is an ACE technique called *cord-cutting,* and it has helped me move past the resentment. For ten minutes every morning, I find a comfortable spot, focus on my breathing, and visualize Brian. When the session begins, I am attached to Brian, by my brain, heart, arms, and legs, my private parts. I can see cords connecting me to him at each of those points. Then, one by one, those cords dissolve. The session is over. The rage is gone. I am left savoring good memories. Once again, life has joy.

***

Sometime in early 2020, my heart rate—even at rest—was racing, and I could not figure out why. I had palpitations in my chest. I had trouble sleeping. Then the blood results came in. "You have post-traumatic stress disorder," my doctor said. But how was that possible? I had been meditating, working out, decreasing my body fat, and increasing muscle. How could I have stress and not *feel* it?

"You have lived like this for years," the doctor said. "But now the stress is at a dangerous level. You cannot allow it to continue."

He prescribed psychotherapy for six straight months and no contact with Brian. He said it was the only way to heal from all those years of control and abuse. The psychotherapy would work to create new neural pathways and new habits.

I shared the diagnosis with Brian.

"How can I change?" he asked in one text. "I had no idea I was hurting you like this!" he said in another. "I will do whatever I can to help."

You can start by seeing how you are the one who caused this. That is what I wanted to say. *You can start by stifling the destructive urges within you, the ones that broke you and, in the process, me.*

But even now, when we are living apart, and Brian is putting on the hard sell of being a man who is willing to change, he continues to show me proof that he is unwilling or incapable of doing so. Like the time he begged me to meet with him so he could profess his love and tell me he didn't want a divorce and, just two fucking hours later, lined up another supply by connecting with someone from his past.

Another time I told Brian, "I don't want you spending time with Jon and Sue. If you want us to work, start there." Yes, he would, he said. He has long known that I do not approve of Jon. If he could keep his word on this one small request of mine, perhaps hope really was not lost.

But last night I drove past Jon's house. Brian's car was parked outside.

"Jon is my friend," Brian said when I mentioned it, "and I needed to talk to him."

Sure you did, Brian. Sigh.

It might be a tiny incongruity, but it is number 99 of the year, and probably the millionth of our entire relationship. When the tiny incongruities are stacked up, it is difficult for me to know what to think.

Brian is very much a situational thinker. I've come to learn there is a term for this. It is called *objective constancy*, and it refers to people for whom the only thing—and the only person—that matters is what or who is in front of them at the moment. This explained why Brian came home from every trip with a story, and why he had to prepare me to see "the pictures"—pictures that would be sent home from girls he met, such as the girl he once told me walked into his room early as he was wrapping up a call. There were other such girls, and other such stories, too numerous for me to recall.

Objective constancy describes Brian perfectly. He says and does whatever is necessary to get what he wants at the moment. He might step into a party holding firmly in his mind every promise of good behavior that he made to me. But when he comes up against temptation, temptation wins every time. "Yes, just once more . . . I'll deal with Kathy later."

Sorry, Brian. Not happening. The cycle has come full circle. Our journey must end.

***

I cannot and will not state that my ex is or ever was a narcissist. I have no idea, information, or belief that he ever received such a diagnosis from a medical professional. I am merely saying here and elsewhere in this book that my ex's actions, behaviors, characteristics, and inclinations tend toward those of narcissists. However, readers should consider my points and judge for themselves.

Divorce is not a matter the narcissist absorbs lightly. They do not concede, cooperate, communicate in a way just for the sake of lessening the blow on the kids, and making everyone affected more comfortable. High conflict remains the strategy, and not far behind it is the still-lurking goal for victory. Entire books have been written to help victims of narcissism survive this traumatic stage of the relationship.

More than just a day of reckoning for the narcissist, who up to this point has enjoyed supreme control over his partner, the divorce also signals his victim's release from bondage. Chances are the narcissist has not found a new partner to manipulate, so he is not about to let his current wife off the hook that easily. "You would think he'd be happy to see me go," said one woman to her therapist. "You're lazy, dumb, not terribly attractive, and can't do anything right. Those were the messages he gave me for years. But now that he finally had a chance to get rid of me, he was holding on for dear life."

This tenacious hold by the narcissist can also have to do with the victim's unique qualities which he finds especially appealing but which he cannot find in others. "I think I am his favorite toy," said one woman. "He plays around, acts like I don't exist, but every now and then he pops back in to make sure his toy is still in the same spot where he left it."

Refusing to accept this final separation, the narcissist is not caving without a fight. A common tactic at this stage is the *fauxpology*. This strategy grows out of the narcissist's lack of genuine feeling and inability to entertain the idea that they could be at fault. A fauxpology neatly and covertly deflects guilt from the narcissist to the partner.

"I'm so sorry that you consider me an utter failure as a husband, a man, a human being," or, "It's a shame that you're so sensitive and don't have a clear picture of this," are typical of the masterful sleights of hand the narcissist will employ. One goes to the farthest extreme by implying that the victim has challenged the narcissist's humanity when, in fact, all the victim has done is to point out destructive behavior that has inflicted pain. Another implies that the victim is a scatter-brained neurotic, unable to make sense of the situation and using the narcissist as a scapegoat for the victim's own flaws.

A particularly outrageous fauxpology expresses utter surprise at the victim's predicament. *OMG, you poor thing. How could this have happened to you?* This type of fauxpology attempts to distance the narcissist from the havoc he has created. When he is presented with evidence of that havoc, he stands back in sheer amazement, as if he is seeing the damage—and even the victim—for the very first time. "It was like walking into a hospital room and seeing a relative who's been in a car crash," said one woman. "Like you're seeing their injuries for the first time. But he was there all along. *He* was the car crash!"

Unless the narcissist has resorted to physical abuse, the wounds that he has inflicted are mostly emotional. This includes pushing the victim, who is trying to free herself from his tentacles, to what therapists call the *hypervigilant state*.

Hypervigilance is the point when a victim of narcissism is drained of physical and emotional strength. Hypervigilance overloads and disables the body's normal defense mechanism. The hypervigilant stage gives way to a deteriorating condition known as complex post-traumatic stress disorder (CPTSD). Note: CPTSD stands for complex post-traumatic stress syndrome and is typical in abusive relationships. PTSD usually occurs after a single traumatic event, while CPTSD is associated with repeated trauma. Yes, the same syndrome that haunts military veterans returning from battle describes the handful of symptoms besieging victims of narcissistic abuse.

It is here, at this point, that the victim needs to disengage. One noted counselor on narcissistic abuse puts it into perspective this way: "Your goal is to get to the place where you are standing outside of the craziness and looking at the narcissist's behaviors more objectively, separating yourself from his or her projections and distorted worldview."

After physical separation comes psychological separation, which is not easy. It is an internal process of re-orientation. It is sometimes likened to the teenager who has outgrown her childhood home and ventures out into the world to begin a new life as an adult.

Psychological separation is a necessary stage for women divorcing narcissistic husbands, but it can be terrifying. These women have for years existed in a cocoon manufactured by the narcissist. They had long ago ditched their sense of self. "I gave up me to be loved by you" is how one best-selling book described the dynamic of women learning to adapt to a narcissist whom they have concluded they could not live without. But now, they no longer dwell in La La Land. Emancipation day is getting close.

Awakened is the word that comes to mind. This stage of awakening is full of both joy and terror. Freeing oneself from a distorted reality requires also that one adopt a new reality. There is no question, though, that it is the most difficult part, described by some as an experience similar to a drug addict's withdrawal. Victims must break from the psychological abuse and traumatic bonding held in place by years of a destructive push-pull relationship. Creating new neural pathways is vital but, in practice, is so much harder than it sounds.

But who am I? The woman wonders, perhaps for the first time since tying the knot. She is suddenly on new ground and feeling anything but grounded.

The journey to answer that question can take months or a lifetime. It begins in the recovery stage with thorough cleansing of the psyche. In order to work on her self-esteem, the victim must rid herself of the narcissist's negative messages that were for years internalized. It is a time of cleaning up the trauma, moving past the grief, finding and rebuilding the authentic self crushed by the narcissist.

It often starts with lists. "I am" a caring mother, a good citizen, a worthy individual, a successful entrepreneur. The lists give way to contemplation. What matters to me? What brings me happiness? What gives me a sense of fulfillment? How do I find meaning in life?

Matters of health, mostly mental, are dealt with next. A fit body supports a vigorous mind. Eating well, getting rest, nurturing the anatomy. Talents and passions also cannot be overlooked at this stage, although the victim has been conditioned to ignore them.

"The best revenge is massive success!" said Frank Sinatra. One therapist uses this quote to exemplify the journey to self. "I am not talking about what you do," she tells clients, "but about who you are. You do not need to make a million dollars, but you want to feel like a million."

***

14

DECONSTRUCTING MY FEELINGS DURING THE MARRIAGE

n this chapter, I'd like to open up more about the feelings I had during the marriage.

But before I do that, please remember that I am not qualified to label my ex as a narcissist. I am completely unaware that he has ever received that diagnosis from any health professional. The statements which follow should be interpreted as my suggestion that my ex's behavior is strikingly similar to that of a narcissist. No more and no less. Readers are encouraged to make their own conclusions.

Rationalization: My intuition always told me something was off or wrong but the toxic behavior was rationalized. My ex always said he loved me. If he says he loves me, then he must love me. At this time, I had a blind eye to his bad behavior.

Denial: My mind would deny the truth with force. I feel it was a way to cope with the pain and truth that deep down I knew but wasn't ready to mentally or emotionally deal with at the time.

Justification: I tried to justify and explain to myself and many friends that asked me "What the hell, why are you still there?" I always convinced myself that staying was the best choice for the moment. I truly believe I stayed not only out of fear of my ex, but also out of fear that, "Would I make it on my own?"

Helplessness: Part of the abusive cycle was to push away responsibility for myself, become helpless, and fully dependent on my ex.

Self-worth, or lack of it, was created in the marriage. My ex would push my self-worth in the wrong direction by manipulating negative thoughts, creating dependency, and an environment in which I would increasingly have more self-doubt and less self-worth. His entire world revolved around his ego for the final years of our marriage.

I lost out on outside relationships. All my friends eventually were his circle of friends. I remember my mom recently commenting that during the first ten years of the marriage, I really wasn't around to see her that much. I never really realized this was the case until it was pointed out, and I really thought about it. Thinking back, I recall there always being small comments made about certain friends or family, comments that made me second guess my decision to go out. There were times too when I was made to feel guilty for going out and leaving him home alone. This was very early in the marriage. He would point out imperfections or things that annoyed him about certain people, again making me second guess and feel guilt through this manipulation and persuading me to feel the same way that he felt.

His sense of entitlement over time would grow, and I was spending more time with him and relying on only him to meet my needs. The more this happened the less time I got to spend with others, and eventually it felt like most relationships were lost. This was early on in the marriage, and I saw it as love, not control.

While feeling completely embraced in the marriage by my ex, it might be hard to understand the gravity of an emotionally abusive relationship. And without outside relationships to help and to recognize, it only got harder.

Low self-esteem: My ex whittled away at my self-esteem. He wanted to maintain his emotional control. He could never, ever admit to being wrong. Ask anyone! That being said, no matter what the actual facts were, I was always wrong, and he was always right. I was criticized outright and in a passive-aggressive manner, and belittled over the entire marriage, and eventually his constant criticism did impact my self-esteem.

I always felt like I was never good enough. Even when I would receive compliments about my appearance, I couldn't accept them because in my mind I believed I "wasn't perfect." Anything less than perfect was a failure. I have come to realize that the constant criticism was really not directed at me but a reflection of how he truly felt/feels about himself on the inside. I believe he, and for that matter anyone who suffers from this disorder or abuses others, is a very insecure little child inside himself. Their goal is to build themselves up and make themselves feel better by bringing others down so they feel better than you and about themselves. No one can measure up to their expectations or themselves. They are better than everyone.

The sense of entitlement is really quite unreal. They thrive on the idea that they are out of your league, that you will not leave them because they have made you believe you are not going to get any better than them. This sense of entitlement in the relationship really has you brainwashed to think that if you leave, you are stupid. It's all steeped into the low self-esteem that was impressed upon me.

I felt sometimes like I was going crazy. After much research, I learned that he was attempting to brainwash and manipulate me. That's what gaslighting is all about. It worked for a good long time. I did doubt myself and lost my sense of perception and self-worth.

My ex lied to me and criticized me non-stop. If I would try to talk about it or call him out on his lies, he would deny it and become defensive. Instead of owning it and accepting responsibility, he would make it sound like I was the one with the problem. I can think of one very specific argument when he outright said, "That didn't happen." Like hell it didn't! It did happen, and I was not going crazy. I kept a journal and confirmed it to him. That was when he ghosted me for four days in February 2020.

As I mentioned in Chapter 12, my ex's gaslighting behavior was repeated so much that it was the reason I started keeping a journal. If I wasn't keeping a journal, then I'm sure I wouldn't be able to defend his questions on my judgment, and I would have to believe his deception.

Being this emotionally abused over time has taken a while to undo. I am still healing, but I see the light at the end of the tunnel. It is important to learn to trust yourself and your instincts before you are able to recognize what an abusive relationship looks like. I was not crazy, and neither are you.

***

There were other feelings during the marriage that I now recall, such as always having to focus on keeping him happy. My life was all about making and keeping him happy, and quite honestly the first years of our marriage, it didn't seem as bad; but I noticed as time went on, if I wasn't feeding his ego and keeping him happy, he would get upset, act like a child, and he even one time said to me that, "He needed me to give him more attention."

He was jealous of ANYONE else getting my attention. His behavior would change, and I would learn to make sure he was given what he wanted, otherwise I might get the cold shoulder or the silent treatment.

I lost myself. Being in an abusive relationship, my life was all about him. Over time, I started to lose myself. The dreams and goals that I had for my own life slowly started to disappear because my ex controlled so much of my life. Everything in my life revolved around him. As I explained above, when I wanted to have a part-time job, he resisted, saying that it would "screw up the taxes." I thought, *Really?*

Arguments always ended with me apologizing, regardless of what the argument was about. As I mentioned earlier, my ex was never wrong in his mind and never, ever accepted accountability for anything, even with proof. (There will be more on that later in this book.) That means, even if you know they were wrong, and they know they were wrong, they will still not apologize. Not ever! Their sense of self-importance will overpower any scenario. Every argument that we had always ended in me taking the blame for it. Everything was my fault. Even things that were outside of my control seemed to get twisted to my doing somehow. "Because you made me mad," was a popular line by my ex.

In an abusive relationship, not only are you criticized physically but for things like grocery shopping, laundry, making lunches. Anything and everything.

When you are treated like this in what is supposed to be a loving relationship, over time the constant criticizing can cause a lot of emotions for you. Some that I experienced were guilt, fear, self-worth, and eventually, resentment.

Over the years there have been so many terrible events that I now look at and wonder, *What was I thinking?* The writing was on the wall, the proof was in the pudding, of more bad behavior, but I always overturned it by ignoring.

Why did I do that?

My research has helped me to understand this scenario a little better. According to Dr. Sharie Stines, PsyD from *GoodTherapy*: "When people are in abusive relationships, they consciously or unconsciously use many coping strategies. In fact, most such coping strategies involve the use of their own strengths such as forgiveness, giving (more than 50% in the relationship), tolerance, patience, accommodation and other pro-social skills for adapting to a difficult situation. Sometimes, though, not so positive traits are used to adapt to an abusive situation. These include minimizing, denial, rationalizing, pretending, anxiety, depression and PTSD, and then there is *abuse amnesia*."

What exactly does abuse amnesia look like? It's when a person has been abused in any way, shape, or form, and in a matter of minutes, hours, or days, it's as if the occurrence of abuse never happened. Both the victims and the abuser carry on as if the incident never happened.

Why does abuse amnesia occur? One reason is brain chemistry. Here are the brain chemicals involved and their effects:

Oxytocin—bonding

Dopamine—craving, pursuing, longing, motivating, saliency

Endogenous opioids—withdraws equals pain, use equals pleasure

Cortisol—stress

Adrenaline—stress

When the abusive incident happens, the hormones cortisol and adrenaline are released, putting the individual in a heightened sense of readiness. After extensive incidents of abuse, the brain response has been familiarized with a pattern: abuse and abandonment, and then relief.

***

During the abandonment phase of the cycle, the victims' brain releases chemicals that cause the feelings of longing, anticipation, and the motivation to find relief. Endogenous opioid withdrawal causes pain, and the neurotransmitter dopamine motivates the person to search for relief in the object of desire, the abuser. Once the chaotic encounter between the victim and abuser is over, homeostasis sets in. The abusive relationship has become a system.

***

All systems strive for homeostasis, which occurs at a state of equilibrium. Each person in the system adjusts in order to reach the "perfect" state of equilibrium. Abuse amnesia is an essential component of this balance.

Here's an example of this in my marriage: I always said I was looking for closure in the marriage. I had it so many times over, but the abuse amnesia prevents you from accepting it as abuse and "forgiving and forgetting."

There were countless situations over the years that I can give as examples for the abuse amnesia, but the one that sticks out the most to me was Brian's trip to Indonesia. I remember it was Saturday, March 11, 2016 at 11:30 a.m. EST, which would have made it 11:30 p.m. his time. I received a pocket dial (I am not sure if it was accidentally on purpose, or not, but most likely it was). This call left a message on my phone of a "party transaction" being arranged with entertainment. He spoke in the message about his antics on another vacation arranging the same scenario.

When I asked my ex about it the next day—because, of course, his phone "went dead" as it did many Saturday nights which, by the way, is an interesting coincidence, wouldn't you say?—his reply was, "It didn't happen." He said he went back to his hotel, "sick that night," and that I made a mistake. "Let me hear the recording," he said. "Nope," I said. I know he wanted to hear it to lie and manipulate me with the words on the message, like everything else he did in the relationship.

I recall speaking with one of his friends that was on this trip with my ex. "He went back to the hotel sick that night," his friend said. Wow! He was so calculated, my ex, that he didn't even tell his friends about his little private party. That is very cunning, wouldn't you say?

***

There were so many red flags over the relationship. Although they were everywhere, emotional manipulation is difficult to spot, particularly in a marriage. Accepting that my husband, who claimed to love me so much, was emotionally manipulating and abusing me was very hard for me to accept.

He was wonderful in the beginning when he needed to be as part of the abusive cycle, but his true face was shown to me only when he knew that I was emotionally invested.

I now know that the first step in protecting myself from manipulation is to know how to recognize it. I have listed five warning signs that I overlooked; these were red flags:

1. Emotional Blackmail: One of the most powerful forms of manipulation is emotional blackmail. My ex made me feel like I was trapped and had no options. "I will make your kids hate you." That statement makes me cringe each time I think of it. He was relying on my fear and my guilt. He also threatened to cheat on me if I didn't do certain things that he wanted from me in the relationship, holding me as an emotional hostage by putting pressure on me to obey him and not at all concerned with my boundaries.

2. He always played the victim, and I have heard that he continues to do so. Research has shown me that most manipulators play the role of the victim. Whatever the situation and whatever the cause, a manipulator will always

find a way to present himself as a victim. He will rarely take responsibility for his words or actions and will always try to make you "wear the hat." This was also the case with my ex. According to him he behaves perfectly, and I was the bad guy who constantly took the heat for any wrongdoings in the relationship. In the rare case that he might admit to doing something wrong, he still tried to convince me that it was me who caused him to behave like that, and then it would be in his eyes fundamentally my fault. My ex would always say in this case, "You made me mad!" He never, ever sincerely apologized. Instead, he constantly tried to justify himself by making me feel guilty for whatever wrongdoing that was happening at any given time.

3. Passive-aggressive behavior: This behavior is never direct, and it is one of the hardest things to spot. Some examples of passive-aggressive behavior might include avoiding direct or clear communication. The communication in our marriage sucked! Not for a lack of trying on my behalf, but for a complete lack on my ex's part. There was never good or any communication in the relationship at all. Other examples of passive-aggressive behavior are: (1) evading problems—yes, he did; (2) making excuses—yes, he did this, too; (3) playing the victim—always!; (4) sarcasm and back-handed compliments—check and check; (5) the silent treatment—*giant check!*

4. He highlights your insecurities: My ex would always target my self-confidence. He could not ever allow me to

be strong and confident because otherwise he would have a hard time controlling me. An example that comes to mind was when I bought this amazing white tropical bikini, and I was excited to wear it. Do you know how hard it is to pull off a white bikini? Anyway, my ex's reaction was: "You know if you lost five pounds, that would look really great on you." Really? That was a perfect example of highlighting my insecurities. If my body and grooming were anything less than perfect, they were unacceptable.

He used my fears and insecurities to make me a victim of his manipulation. My ex was a very competent manipulator and was able to recognize my insecurities and bring them out whenever he needed to put me down.

Patronizing and belittling me was subtle at first but over time became very apparent. Remarks such as calling me a "loser" when I first opened my studio and wanted to turn a profit during the first year. This was another case when I was looking for an apology and the old "you made me mad" excuse was laid.

Insults disguised as jokes? This was another common issue with my ex. Who's laughing at the fact that I think I'm overweight when it's only you and I in the room? Who was that joke meant for? Enough said.

Before you know it, these tactics start to convince the victim they are good for nothing and that the abuser is doing you a favor by staying with you.

The manipulator behaves this way because he is afraid you will see his true intentions and that you will leave him, so he wants to reduce your self-esteem to the bare minimum. Therefore you end up believing that no other man would want you, and you continue your relationship with the manipulator.

5.   He confuses your mind—playing with your head and making you doubt your sanity. This is one of the successful forms of manipulation that any skilled abuser uses. This manipulation technique will always distort what you say and try to present a reality different from what the reality really is. (This is called gaslighting, and I have discussed this at length, above). The abuser tries to alter your view of history or an event to suit his lies or behavior. Over time this behavior is completely exhausting, and you will begin to doubt your perception of reality and will end up believing everything he says because you THINK you are going crazy. That is the idea behind this technique: you are now his ideal supply.

***

The song "Someone Else" hits many cords with me. No one, and I mean no one, truly knew my ex and his behavior/character like I did.

"I wake up in the bed you made
the one where you are supposed to lay with me
I smell you on the pillowcase

but don't see your face, and that's okay with me

I never thought I'd see the day
I'd see you as somebody I could hate
I guess that's just the price I pay
for the blood red flags that I walked by everyday

Chorus:

Who are you when I'm not looking?
You're like an angel sent from hell
Despite those eyes that hooked me
When I'm not looking, you are someone else

Hey
Is it me? Did I fly you away?
Am I wrong? Are you not who I say?
If I call which one of you will answer Anyway?

15

STAGES OF RECOVERY IN AN EMOTIONALLY AND PSYCHOLOGICALLY ABUSIVE RELATIONSHIP

would like to point out, once again, that there was no diagnosis for my ex and that I am not qualified to provide one. However, his personal characteristics, along with his behavior and the abusive situations he subjected me to, all bear an uncanny resemblance to those most commonly associated with the narcissist personality.

My healing and recovery process has not been linear. It has always felt as though I were taking two steps forward and then one step back. I have had to constantly question myself, more so in the beginning of the healing process. I also blamed myself, experienced guilt, and endured downright emotional meltdowns. I had to keep reminding myself that the abusive relationship I suffered through happened because I am a caring, kind, and loving person who always chooses to find the good in others, particularly in those whom I think love me. However, it turned out that I was undermined and invalidated in my marriage. No one deserves abuse. No one. And everyone deserves to find love and true intimacy and to be acknowledged in their relationships.

I experienced shock and denial. It was hard to accept that the ex whom I loved so much could show narcissistic tendencies, so I denied it. I told myself that underneath all those flaws, my ex really did love me. Perhaps, I thought, I just needed to try harder. Perhaps then he would give me the love and attention that I craved and deserved.

At first I was very reluctant to admit even to myself that my ex was an undiagnosed but textbook character of a narcissist. After all, we had been together practically our entire lives. He was affectionate most of the time, and certainly at the beginning of our relationship and at the end, when he suspected I was going to leave.

Next came pain and guilt. As I really started to recognize and pay attention to my ex's traits, I would blame myself for not seeing past the manipulation. The pain of having spent so much time and energy trying to make the relationship with him work. I have to mention that each time my ex and I separated, not even once was he the one to fix things, to make amends to change. It was always me. There are times when I look back at the marriage and think, *I wasted so much time with him.*

And what about those red flags? Did I really miss all of them? How could I be so stupid? I was always trying to please him. I wasted so much emotion, love, and time on someone who didn't really care about me.

Part of my healing process was to try to understand that I was not capable of accepting all the events and bad behavior that happened during the marriage until I was emotionally strong enough. I also understand now that part of the incredible strength and resilience that I have today is the result of the relationship warfare that I walked through which has made me feel like a fucking warrior! It made me who I am today. It gave me the foundation of my purpose in the world, so for that, I say, "Ex, thank you!"

The next stage in healing involved anger and bargaining. I am angry that my ex misled and manipulated me, but had I just tried a little harder, maybe that would have changed. I was always telling myself that this latest incident could be the last. Truth is, I didn't want to leave because, I told myself, this time he will regret losing me and that will make him change. I really believed that if I kept sacrificing my own needs for his, I would somehow get the love I deserved.

As I went further into this journey of marriage, I became more angry and more resentful. I now understand those feelings were actually very healthy, but then I would find myself slipping back into "hope mode," which usually meant I was trying to get my ex to change. For years, I begged him to change his partying ways.

I now also understand that people with this personality disorder will not change unless there is something in it for them. My ex did not and would not change, even when the threat of divorce was presented to him. Whenever his partying ways caused upset in the relationship, his initial reaction was "Yes it's the last time . . . I won't do it again." But that sentiment only lasted until the next time, which was usually only a few days or no more than a week away.

Another stage of recovery had me going through depression, flexion , and loneliness.

I had been loving and compassionate. Yet I was continually being manipulated and betrayed. I felt like he had exploited my vulnerability. He left me feeling empty. I realize now that he never loved me.

Sooner or later, the realization came that ours wasn't a loving relationship at all. I believe there are four pillars that make for a lasting intimate relationship. Those are: love, respect, trust, and honesty. Unfortunately, my marriage with my ex failed on all four.

16

THE LESSONS I LEARNED

I have learned a lot about feeling and emotions in this past year.

A big lesson is summed up by this quote that I came across:

"The more chances you give someone to hurt you the less respect they'll start to have for you. They'll take advantage of your forgiveness. They won't be afraid to lose you because they think you will never walk away. Never let a person get comfortable with disrespecting you."

I learned that throughout the marriage, I was suffering from emotional numbness. I remember hearing some tragic news about a friend whom I love dearly. That news should have brought heartbreak, pain, and tears to me, as it would to any normal caring human. Yet, it did not. I recall having felt completely numb. Did I even care that my dear friend fell on hard times? Of course I did! But I couldn't feel anything.

Here is an example from the time I decided to step back and close my studios in order to focus all of my time and energy on me. It was Christmas Eve, and the last class at my studio finished at 10 a.m. We had developed such an incredible community at the studios. There was so much inspiration, love, and support. The coaches were in tears, the clients were in tears. I thanked everyone, gave them well wishes and a happy holiday message and did not shed one tear. That was another time I remember feeling completely numb. Again, it isn't that I did not care. Rather, I felt numb because I had consciously stripped myself of emotion, putting myself in numb feeling survival mode, just to cope with my marriage. At the time, I remember a good friend recognizing this. "I can tell you are having difficulty," she said to me. "There is no sparkle in your eyes. The average person can't tell because you are smiling as though everything is great, but I can see the truth in your eyes."

***

"Love is many things, but it is never deceitful.
Nothing toxic comes from genuine love."

***

I have learned that true love shouldn't be hard. It should be easy. Let me be clear, I am not referring to words spoken, but to action and behavior. I don't mean that there aren't issues that arise in any relationship. Of course there are, but love is not selfish, controlling, lacking in respect, unreliable, irresponsible, immature, manipulative, or emotionally unavailable. Love should never feel heavy and painful. Love is honest, respectful, loyal, selfless, trustworthy, joyful, peaceful, and harmonious, and the most fucking incredible feeling a human can ever experience.

I learned an important lesson about the silent treatment. Being ghosted is the worst psychological aggression one human can advance on another. Ghosting is equivalent to murder . . . not physical murder but certainly emotional murder. My ex sometimes denied my existence, inflicting on me the highest punishment one can inflict mentally on another person. Did you know that being ignored by a loved one causes the same chemical reaction in the brain as a physical injury?

I learned that my ex never really loved me, and that's because he never loved himself. Perhaps he loved the idea of me, the idea of how I made him feel. It is an unpleasant and cruel part of my healing process from the abuse that I am forced to admit this. I wasn't even in a real loving relationship. It was more like a MANIPULATIONSHIP. This type of person is not capable of love nor do they seek it. They seek supply of our efforts and gifts and they seek to control others and in that control, they find peace If you even once question their actions or challenge them, you quickly become the enemy, and thus begin the bullying and tantrums.

I learned to love the words that are spoken to me but to ensure they are matched with like behavior patterns. If not, it's best to beware of the red flags. They are the true character of the abuser.

This is a good point to ponder the truth of this quote, the truth of which is like a punch to the gut:

"How they treat you is how they feel about you . . . Period."

How's that for a life-changing lesson?

I have learned that abusers and narcissists will try to destroy their victims' lives with lies because they know theirs can be destroyed with the truth. The smear campaign is a very real thing. Since I have left the marriage and my ex can no longer control me, he is trying to control the way others see me. They try to destroy and discredit anyone who sees them for who they really are. They know that anyone who sees through their mask could expose them, so they will stop at nothing to make sure it doesn't happen. I have chosen not to engage. I have chosen to take the high road.

***

"Never sacrifice your class to get even with someone who has none. Let them have the gutter, you take the high road.

***

I have learned that I was never crazy. But I was abused to believe that I was crazy. A lot of times outsiders see those that are victims of emotional/psychological abuse and narcissism as "crazy" or dramatic. As a victim of abuse, I was subjected to many years of gaslighting in combination with a very strategic smear campaign that started as the marriage came closer and closer to the finish. Everything a narcissist does is calculated to achieve some goal. Their life is a well-thought-out chess game with every move a calculated one. Again, I must stress that my ex was never diagnosed with narcissistic personality disorder. However, how he acted, and how he lived his life, and how I was treated are a carbon copy of actions associated with this disorder.

I learned a great deal from having returned to the marriage over and over again. I was made to feel that not only was I not good enough to survive on my own, but that I was missing something. It is now one year after the marriage has ended, and this is what I know: that I have recovered from my physical signs of CPTSD, extreme stress, insomnia, an unhealthy high resting heart rate, high cortisol levels in my blood work, and many other unhealthy markers. Those were the symptoms that told my doctor everything about my emotional well-being without me ever having to utter one word (even if he already knew the entire story!)

My body fat is an optimal 25.1 percent, zero inflammation. I have zero health concerns. All bloodwork markers are optimal. Ensuring that one achieves internal healing after abusive relationships is necessary for the outside healing to stick.

I have also learned, quite happily, that I can love and trust others again. And it feels like nothing I have ever felt before in my life. I kind of like it!

Oh yes, and I finally realize that with the help of my psychotherapists, I was missing something. I was missing a loving, trusting, honest, caring relationship and husband that I thought I had in my marriage.

This was perhaps the hardest pill to swallow, but I also learned that I was in love with a lie. The person I fell in love with never existed. My ex created this character just for me. He saw how amazing I was, and he copied my characteristics.

I also learned that everything is my fault. Yes, I place 100 percent of the blame on myself. I went forward, even though I recognized the red flags, which often reveal a person's true self, much more so than their words. I am grateful for all the lessons that I learned in my marriage, and the drama, and storms that I survived, because it has made me into this incredibly strong woman who is completely resilient AF (as fuck), and I wouldn't change the person I am now or the woman I have become for anything.

I once read that, "It takes grace to remain kind in cruel situations." I heartily agree.

While we're on the subject of grace, here's another salient quote:

"When you learn that a person's behavior has more to do with their own internal struggle than it ever did with you . . . you learn grace."

I have chosen to look upon my ex in a way that does not judge him for how he treated me. Rather, if he does indeed have a narcissistic personality disorder, I feel compassion for him. I hope that my readers will consider the examples I have given and perhaps even do their own research.

Narcissism starts in childhood. The onset of pathological narcissism is in infancy, childhood, and early adolescence. It is commonly attributed to childhood abuse and drama inflicted by parents or their authority figures. Pathological narcissism is a defense mechanism intended to deflect hurt and drama from the victim's *true self* into a *false self* which is omnipotent, invulnerable, and omniscient. The narcissist uses the false self to regulate his or her labile sense of self-worth by extracting from his environment narcissistic supply (any form of attention both positive and negative).

I know through the many stories of my ex and other family members that my ex's mother also exhibited narcissistic tendencies and inclined toward emotional and psychological abuse. Again, I am not qualified to make a medical diagnosis in that regard. I am merely pointing out that some of her characteristics are those of narcissists. I also came to that conclusion on my own and did so after observing her behaviors throughout my marriage. I know that she, too, was raised by an abusive father who displayed characteristics of the classic narcissist.

Again, I am not labeling my husband as a narcissist. I don't know if any doctor or other healthcare professional has ever done so. I am suggesting only that his behaviors and characteristics during my decades-long relationship with him overlap with those of the traditional narcissist. Readers of this book are encouraged to consider that disclaimer and judge for themselves.

Knowing what I now know about this terrible condition truly breaks my heart. Anyone suffering from this at a very delicate age in childhood needs some type of intervention. Where I once had so much anger, pain, sadness, and resentment in my heart, I now feel nothing but love, acceptance, forgiveness, understanding, and compassion for the emptiness these people have inside. They are empty shells. Instead of passing judgement from my view, I have found forgiveness to be much easier. I now view my ex not from the position of a wife who was hurt constantly in the relationship, but rather from the eyes of a higher power.

I have learned that *no contact* is a very necessary part of the healing process. When my doctor suggested no contact with my ex, along with six months of psychotherapy, as an option for treatment, I was hesitant. I truly believed that I wanted to continue the marriage and was hoping this was the answer. The doctor told me I was in a unique situation since most victims do not choose to continue with their abuser after they have decided on no contact. Little did I realize that my reaction to this was not because of love but actually because of an attachment created by trauma bonding, which I have discussed earlier.

Let me quickly educate you on the difference between love and attachment: attachment is about fear and dependency and has more to do with love of self than love of another. Love without attachment is the purest love because it doesn't assume you are empty and isn't about what others can give you. It is about what you give to others because you are already full.

Love is free, flexible, patient, kind, trusting, confident, content, generous, and understanding. By contrast, attachment is clinging, inflexible, impatient, unkind, jealous, insecure, craving, selfish, and greedy.

Those facts remind me of a quote I recently heard: *"A woman can't change a man because she loves him, a man changes himself because he loves her!"*

What is the purpose and science behind no contact? First, let me clarify what I mean by no contact. What I mean is there cannot be any contact—direct or indirect—with the abuser. There should be no texts, emails, phone calls, no dropping off food at my door, no notes through the kids . . . *no contact.*

How did my ex, the abuser, feel about my having to deny him contact? I'm sure he had feelings similar to what a drug addict feels when facing withdrawal. In that sense, the narcissist is like a drug addict. He is addicted to attention, admiration, praise, and control. This is what psychologists refer to as *narcissistic supply.* Narcissists must always have some sort of supply. They need distractions from their own internal pain. What happens then? They will hoover and try to pursue their main supply (in this case, it was me) in an attempt to persuade them that no contact isn't going to help anyone, or they will look for secondary supply (others) while their main supply heals from the abuse they caused.

In case you are wondering why and how no contact helps victims, let me explain. One who leaves an abusive marriage isn't helped by merely shutting off her phone, focusing on other people in her life, telling others about the pain she endured, or returning to old hobbies and finding new ones to keep herself occupied. None of that will work if she hasn't mentally left the abuser.

Quite literally, victims must shift perspective away from what they thought was real. They must cultivate a new understanding of reality in order to successfully leave the abuser once and for all. This cannot be done overnight. In my case, it started to happen when I was still in the marriage. Even though the marriage has been over for just about a year, I checked out mentally many years before that. I was always holding onto the belief that I couldn't leave just in case he happened to change, just in case he happened to be the one who was right. This stage usually occurs while our brains are chemically addicted to the abuse cycle that has been perpetrated by the narcissist's actions.

Here is some science about this type of abuse. Psychological trauma shrinks the hippocampus and prefrontal cortex of the brain, activating our fight, flight, or freeze response and making it difficult to make sound decisions that are not based on the drama-manufactured emotion. When I discovered the science of why I couldn't physically leave the marriage, I no longer felt helpless and had hope that I could heal and turn my life around. It was not easy for me to get to this stage of no contact with my ex in the marriage, let alone try to maintain no contact once it was prescribed by my doctor.

The abuser knows by the time you have initiated the no contact rule that you have figured them out. Does that stop them from the continued manipulation and mind games? Hell no. For my entire relationship with Brian, I was his conditioned supply. While I was in my no contact period, and he was well aware I was onto his true self, the constant hoovering on his behalf disguised as caring gestures was something I could never get away from. These were more examples of his manipulations and also of the pull that was designed to bring me back into the abusive cycle.

Any victim in no contact mode must ignore the abuser at all times. Once a victim goes no contact, they feel worse (at least at the beginning of the no contact) than they did while they were in the relationship. The victim can feel like a heroin addict going cold turkey.

As I tried to maintain no contact, I wanted to go back to my ex in the worst way because I was feeling the fear, the pain, and the sadness. I was addicted to the emotions that I had been feeling while I was in the abusive relationship. It's a simple chemical process. That's why victims simply have to accept what has happened to them. They must walk through that emotional shit storm and just allow themselves to feel it all.

There are many times when a victim is healing that the abuser will come back and destroy or try to destroy all the effort they've put into healing. The abuser tries guilt trips and manipulations to lure the victims back, and they do it so they can hurt the victim all over again. The abuser will promise the victim that things this time around will be different and better. But that is a lie. Things never get better. They always get worse because the second and third times around the abuser wants to penalize the victim for attempting to leave.

This is what I learned about the stage when the abuser realizes that they have lost to no contact. From my own no contact period, I observed that my ex said he supported whatever methods I needed in order to heal but, in fact, he was messaging another woman at the same time, likely to line up another supply in anticipation of me leaving. I also noticed how he made sure he had to be the one to announce the ending of the marriage. In private, I told him I was out, done, through with the marriage for good. In public, he had to appear as the victim who couldn't take any more. I have seen this many times throughout the marriage: in the stories he told about our marriage, he was either the hero or the victim, but he was never the villain. And even as I adhered to my doctor's no contact prescription, there were many push-pull attempts that were always apparent. My ex's words became stronger, as he tried to suck me back in. However, his behavior didn't change.

17

MY CLOSURE

"A person who truly values you won't ever put themselves in a position to lose you."

Ask any victim of a narcissistic-abusive relationship what is the hardest thing for them to find, and you will discover the most common response is closure. This book has touched upon many events from my life that would be considered closure by those who have never been the victims of abuse. However, I found myself having to move past these events, having to hold on still, hoping for real closure.

Well, my instincts were right. I knew it had to be out there, somewhere. And I did end up finding it. There it was, in my ex's emails. He responded to a random online hookup. It wasn't spam. It was his bona fide reply to meet up with "Lisa."

For me, that was it. That was all the closure I needed.

***

"Revenge isn't in my plans, you will fuck yourself on your own."

***

Although I have described my relationship as narcissistic, I am again emphasizing that I am not certified to make that conclusion or to diagnose my ex as a narcissist. This chapter and every other in this book are intended only to compare my ex's behavior with that of the classic narcissist. In that regard, readers must come to their own opinions.

18

THE AFTERMATH

"I was abused quietly so I choose to heal loudly."

Before I discuss the aftermath, I would like to remind readers that I am not labeling my ex as a narcissist. I am not qualified to do that. Nor do I have any information that he has ever been labeled as such by one who is qualified to make that determination. Please construe my statements here and on every other page of this book as my attempt to compare my ex's behavior with that of the typical narcissist.

Recovery after a narcissistic-abusive relationship is a gradual process. There must be time to navigate. In my case, at the least, it required six straight months of psychotherapy that was needed to remove the subconscious complex and ingrained beliefs, habits, thoughts, and emotions that had built up over all those years.

More importantly, it was vital that I complete each phase of the process. I could not allow myself to get stuck. I could not afford to take even one shortcut, just as one would not think to take a shortcut while going through the grieving process.

My journey to healing started when I went no contact. An important first step was the realization and acceptance that my marriage had in fact been abusive. I became very aware of the physical and emotional dangers that faced me should I stay in the relationship. For those who have not experienced a manipulative relationship, it can be truly difficult to explain the psychological and emotional complexities that are involved in snaring a victim into a narcissistic bond. As I have said before, experts in the field have compared the victim who tries to break away from a narcissistic relationship to "a drug addict going through painful withdrawals when they can't have their fix."

My healing journey has consisted of me taking care of myself—physically, nutritionally, mindfully, emotionally. It involved me surrounding myself with supportive friends and family. During this process, I have noticed physical changes that have more to do than just shrinking body fat and increasing muscle. There have been controlled internal body markers for optimal proactive health. Still, it is truly incredible that once we open ourselves up and truly experience our own worth, even our sexuality and sexual experiences rise to a whole new level.

19

THE IRON GODDESS CODE

was typing away at the final chapter of this book when it occurred to me that I hadn't yet thought of a title. I had some vague ideas, of course. I knew that it would have to capture, in a nutshell, the gist of my story, a true account of one woman's awakening to inner strength. It would be neat, I thought, if I could find a title that fit the logo on the back of this book, which shows a woman walking out of the fire she's clearly left in the dust. That logo captures the drama I've lived and the way I'm feeling now.

That's when it occurred to me. Why not use the name of my rebranded studio, The Iron Goddess, and call this book *The Iron Goddess Code?* When people hear the word iron, they associate it with fitness, pumping weights, and lifting, and that's all true. But to me, there's a deeper meaning in that word.

I think of iron as representing a strong will, a determined spirit, a forceful inner drive not unlike the drive I was able to conjure up after decades of emotional torment that left me drained and downhearted. To me, iron symbolizes the inner power that any woman can muster when she finds herself in the middle of a storm.

Yes, I told myself, *The Iron Goddess Code* would be perfect. It aptly describes my mission in rebranding the studio. That mission is to help my clients, mostly women, understand that they're in control of whatever is going on around them.

What brought me to the word goddess? Another no-brainer. Goddess is what every woman has inside. It's the ability to tap into your best confidence, your strongest self, the power to fight back.

Tapping into my inner goddess is something I started several months ago with a surprising diagnosis. "You have post-traumatic stress disorder," my doctor said, then instructed me to avoid contact—*any contact*—with the people who'd abused me. He said that I needed to heal from decades of emotional and verbal abuse, and the no contact rule was the only way to begin the healing process. Let's ponder why that is so.

Consider a long-term abusive relationship, the kind that pits partner against partner in a type of push-pull struggle. These are the relationships in which an abuser's bad behavior pushes a victim who is struggling, or pulling, as she tries to handle the abuse. Therapists say that these relationships involve trauma bonding, which is a later stage in the typical narcissistic relationship. The trauma part of that term refers to the fact that couples in these relationships alternate between cycles of rewards and punishments. The bonding part refers to the deep emotional attachment each partner has to such a neurotic relationship. A key feature of trauma bonding is that the behaviors go through a cycle which, by the way, makes it next to impossible for the victim to break free.

Trauma bonding involves one partner manipulating the other through a reward system. It's like rewarding a dog that has performed a trick. He's given a treat. The dog is happy with the treat and longs for another. That's why he can be counted on to do the trick again, in effect, to repeat the cycle.

The same phenomenon happens in humans who are rewarded for doing something well. Like the dog, the human is giddy with the reward. It gives them a dopamine rush. When the rewards come in the context of a narcissistic relationship, they're doled out whenever there is drama, whether it is abuse or love. The dopamine fix is high because the victim never knows what to expect or when to expect it. But until that reward comes, the victim staggers in a state of high anticipation, the dopamine rushing like water pounding through a stream.

The longer that this trauma bonding goes on, the harder it will be for a victim to leave the relationship. If and when the victim is finally able to break free, she is still likely to be in a compromised psychological condition, prone to the symptoms a drug addict experiences during withdrawal.

This cyclic pattern and the resulting bond that it creates are intense, immeasurably so. That is precisely why victims are warned to maintain no contact in the initial stages of separation from an abusive partner. It truly is a crucial first step in freeing oneself from bondage to a narcissist.

In my situation, leaving and breaking the trauma bond would be a process, not a simple act you perform once. Even as I knew I had to leave, that nothing would change from my ex, and it was actually a matter of my life and death, I also had painful empty feelings as I broke the trauma bond with the no contact order from my doctor. I can recall how terrible it was. It is harder than a drug addict trying to get off of hard drugs. I was always looking for my next hit of dopamine...never to find it.

To appreciate the significance of no contact, we need to consider that even after a relationship ends, many couples remain in limited contact. This means that a victim anticipates receiving messages from an abuser. Victims of narcissistic relationships, in particular, look forward to those messages. Anticipating them often spikes the victim's emotions, the familiar emotions, the same emotions the victim felt during the relationship, even when it was on rocky ground. These emotions include guilt, sadness, anger, confusion, rejection, and even the longing for a reconciliation.

These emotions are triggered by the mere thought of contact with the abuser and all are harmful. These emotions place the victim back in the same diminished position they held during the relationship, the same position they were in as they practiced the old habits and experienced the neural pathways of victimhood. If a victim remains in this vulnerable position, they cannot break away or begin to heal.

The only true road to healing is through no contact. This means cutting all ties and reminding oneself that the relationship is over and there is no going back. It means blocking the narcissist's text messages and social media posts, not calling the narcissist or accepting his calls, refusing any invitations to meet him in public or in private, and avoiding any other possible methods of communication with him. No contact requires women to call forth their inner goddess.

When a victim follows the no contact rule, her mind returns to its normal, healthy state, and her spirit begins to soar. No contact gives trauma bonds time to heal from the abuse. For perhaps the first time in years, a victim has room to grieve, and that leads to healing from every unhealthy bond formed during the relationship.

I am speaking from experience when I say that the no contact rule can bring life-altering benefits. After the first month of my refusing to communicate with a long-term abuser, I was able to meditate and to think with more clarity. For the first time in what seemed like years, I could sit down and focus on my studio, the membership, any business task at hand, and I was once again productive. I'd made clarifying choices.

Of course, I wasn't off the hook just yet; there is still more healing to be done, and I'm still striving for it. As I write these words, about six months after my doctor's recommendation, my very high resting heart rate of 67 beats per minute (bpm) had dropped down to a normal 55 bpm. Not a win to sneeze at.

Once I started to feel even the slightest benefits of no contact, I was hooked. I went looking for other adjustments I could make. Surely there were more; the abusive relationships had seeped into every part of my life. It would take more than just creating physical distance from my abusers to make me feel whole again, to give life to me.

Remember that clarity of mind I talked about earlier? I decided that I wanted more of it in my new life. I did some research and learned that mental clarity feeds off of mental stability, positive psychology, spiritual energy. I learned also that our mental and emotional selves are connected to the spaces where we choose to live. It seems that those spaces have an energy all their own, depending on the people and events our minds associate with them. For me, the apartment I've lived in since late 2019 is no longer the safe haven that it once was. It's actually filled with toxic energy. So I will soon be moving out.

I detected that same toxic energy in a trailer at the beach that I've had for years and where I've recently been doing a lot of work. For me, the beach has always been a source of peace and calm. But the trailer brought back memories of one particularly abusive relationship, of many arguments, and of a night in late summer when I'd been left stranded. The images from that time and the negative emotions filled my mind, no matter how hard I tried to break free from the abuser. The trailer was triggering emotions that could cause me to break down, lose my resolve, and try to communicate with an abuser. Like the apartment, I will leave the trailer and move on to another space. I'm thankful to be able to do that.

***

"Toxic people condition you to believe the problem isn't the abuse itself, but instead your reactions to their abuse."

***

Reminder: I am not qualified to diagnose my ex as a narcissist. I do not intend my statements to be construed as such. However, I am pointing out the similarities between my ex's behavior and that of most narcissists. Readers should consider my points and this disclaimer and come to their own judgments.

***

One of the main reasons I wrote this book was to shine light on healing, because that really is the goal. Healing is such a general term. Many of you may be asking, what does healing look like? How does it make us feel? When can we be assured that we have achieved it?

When I think of healing, I first think of being able to sleep at night and wake up rested. Healing is confidence.

It's being able to look in the mirror and tell ourselves that we are worthy, beautiful, successful, amazing. Healing is the ability to focus on nutrition and whatever it takes to make ourselves better. It's having the strength to read an email from a lawyer's office or an ex and to respond, which involves clear thinking and resilience, rather than to react, which involves stress. For me, healing means that I'm free from the worry. I no longer care what an ex is doing, how he is living or managing without me, whether he will shoot off another text and what it will say. Above all, healing allows mental focus, and I need that. I need to be one hundred percent focused on what I'm doing and where I'm headed.

Healing came gradually. I worked out, meditated, stayed away from my abuser, and, believe it or not, dabbled in hypnosis. I'd heard that hypnotherapy was a way to revisit certain memories and events but not with the goal of returning to that place and time, or to that guy. Rather, hypnosis put me into a trance-like focus. I had intense concentration on some of the more painful events in my past, and this time I came out the winner. With hypnosis, I was able to forgive my younger self for making bad choices. I know to some that might sound crazy, but hypnosis definitely works. I was hooked.

Healing is like a journey that never ends. The abuse I've suffered for far too many years has left me with deep emotional scars, and I've come to accept that they are permanent. For example, I still grapple with how best to receive negative messages, the ones that used to stop my younger self dead in my tracks. Today, tapping into my inner goddess, I'm ready for those negative messages; they are bumps in the road that might make me pause, but they won't derail me.

So the healing continues to restore my inner strength in ways that even I can't always measure. Just in the last six months, I've been impressed with my ability to step back and look at the bad relationships from a healthy distance. This skill has been invaluable. I've learned that the bad relationships weren't a reflection on me but on a narcissistic partner's tormented self-image. That was another tiny step in the healing process, but it took me to others, deeper and more rewarding. Healing has that domino effect.

Healing requires forgiveness. I couldn't end this book without that key message. For me, forgiveness was a stepping stone to my awakened self. I realized that I'd been holding on to so much resentment over the past. Meditation allowed me to see events in a different light and sometimes from another person's perspective. The point is to try to understand what motivates people to do and say certain things. Maybe the best way to explain it is to say that instead of viewing events from my eyes only, I've learned to look down on them from God's eyes. How would God view this person? That non-judgmental, more loving perspective shows how I am now trying to live my life. It's helped me to forgive and to move on.

I've also changed my journaling habits. Funny, perhaps, yet understandable, is that I used to keep a journal of bad behavior. But I've now switched to a journal of gratitude, which is at the front and center of my morning ritual. I spend seven minutes each day writing down what I am thankful for, the big and the small. My children, my family, the friends and clients who've formed a support group for me. And yes, the bad relationships too. They're part of the gratitude. I truly am thankful to my ex and all the soul-changing lessons from this toxic relationship, because all have blended into the new stronger me.

Healing is infectious. Feeling invigorated, fortified, more focused; I couldn't imagine not sharing the experience with my clients. Many clients will remember that I closed Climaxx Studio to focus on me, but the closing was a temporary measure. It was always my intention to reopen Climaxx with a new look and a new system.

The rebranded studio reflects my journey to self-knowledge over the past year or so. In the studio, clients can still expect the fitness and nutrition, the focus on physical health they've come to expect.

But online, there is a membership experience like no other. TheIronGoddess.com will tackle the internal work. By internal, I mean the rituals that immerse us in healthy habits, the most important one being able to resist that glass of wine that we women turn to for solace. Online members of The Iron Goddess will learn that contrary to lifting spirits, alcohol is really a huge downer on the central nervous system. It wreaks havoc on the hormones, causing women in particular to end up more depressed than ever. I know this for a fact; it wasn't too long ago that I also reached for wine to soothe my nerves at the end of long days.

We also teach control, which starts with the simple edict, "Don't hit snooze." Women are in control when they set their alarm, set their intentions, and when the alarm goes off, they get up and start their daily rituals. "Don't hit snooze" is super simple and works to get us started on adding all the other habits that make us feel amazing, since feeling amazing is what we all were designed for. Feeling amazing puts us in control.

We don't stop there. Next at the TheIronGoddess.com, we do meditation, the cord-cutting type that helps women imagine they are removing the strings that bind them to the negative. There is also paradigm shifting, which teaches women to question the fundamental beliefs about themselves that they've held for years. Imagine, for example, a woman who's been told her entire life that she is heavy, and she's believed it. In her mind, the word "heavyset" describes her but not in a positive way. It doesn't enhance her self-esteem. With paradigm shifting, she learns to challenge that self-description and to let go of it, to pursue what she *can be* rather than what she's been taught to believe she is.

All of this internal work is available through the Iron Goddess Membership and anyone can sign up by going to my website, TheIronGoddess.com. The site features real-life stories about my personal struggles through decades of narcissistic relationships. I've even put together an Iron Goddess Manifesto, which can be said as part of a daily meditation. The Manifesto inspires women to create self-care rituals, cultivate their resilience, and have the confidence to move forward in all areas of their lives. Resistance, which too often is regarded as fear, is quite powerful. The Manifesto encourages women to embrace resistance and to view it as change, because change is where the magic happens.

Sign on at TheIronGoddess.com and find the real you. Here's the deal.

We start at your core. We clear the mental fog, the messages from your mother about that too-light-in-color prom dress that won't hide your top-heavy figure, the disapproving looks from your pious aunts, the shame. We banish "can't do" from your vocabulary.

You arrive at your inner goddess and . . .

. . . You walk with a spring in your step. You imagine yourself pampered. You don't overthink buying that snug-fitting size six skirt. You call that guy you met on the subway, the one who gave you his number, the one who couldn't take his eyes off your legs. You sizzle with excitement every time you say his name, feel the wrap of his arms, fantasize the next rendezvous. You begin to lose the guilt. You get naked.

What's next?

Your inner goddess roars. You revel in the images: pumping that iron, rowing past the finish line, crushing that new challenge at the office, finishing that novel, taking in that sunrise, doing your best work yet. Look in the mirror and be dazzled.

Lose yourself just long enough to live for the moment, in the moment. Then circle back to your inner goddess and love her all over again.

The future? It is a blank slate waiting for you to paint it. You choose the landscape and the colors. Peaceful pastels or fiery reds.

Rock it!

***

Note: There are many more self-improvement techniques on TheIronGoddess.com. I accept requests for speaking engagements and one-on-one coaching and mentoring. Those are available at KathyBrodeur.com.

EPILOGUE: A FIERCE NEW FREEDOM

My life is aggressively moving forward in a very fierce and driven way. I continue to fuel my body with healthy and nutritious choices and to move my body every single day. As I write these words, my resting heart rate is down to 50 bpm and my body fat percent is an optimal 25.1 percent. I have gained seven pounds of muscle and . . . I feel *incredible!*

Having successfully completed the six months of psychotherapy prescribed by my family doctor, I can truly say that I have walked through this storm and felt every fucking emotion that was thrown at me. But I came out on the other side of a situation intended to destroy me. Truly, I am a survivor.

I cannot explain—much less fathom—how much pain I endured every step of the way, but I am proud to say that I did it. I prevailed. My triumph was by no means a given. There were times I didn't know if I could do it, but I did know that I could not go back to a life where I did not value myself and where I, in turn, was neither valued nor loved. Like a drug addict kicking his seemingly unconquerable heroin habit, I left an abusive relationship once and for all.

Yes, I fucking did it!

I have said before in this book that I am truly thankful for my ex and for all the experiences and situations he dragged me through. I hope my readers believe this. I'm grateful because his abuse made me strong as fuck! I am more resilient and a much stronger person than I ever thought I would be. So again, I am shouting out to my ex: Thank you, thank you . . . and I say that with nothing in my heart but love.

The abuse has not only made me stronger; it's allowed me to discover my purpose in this world. For years, I'd known that my purpose was to help people, and I have done that through the fitness and nutrition education offered at my studios. But, having gone through an abusive few decades with my ex, I've discovered an even bigger purpose for me: to work internally on myself and to help others with this internal work. The reason—which I have said above but which bears repeating—couldn't be more clear: no matter how you improve the outside, it will not take hold unless you have revamped the inside.

My intention in writing this book is not to extract revenge or to cause pain. It is only to help others recognize abusive patterns in any type of relationship. If I can reach just one person, then I will feel as though my mission has been accomplished.

I've got just one chance at life, and I need to make sure the remaining years are right. I need to give them my best shot. For me, that means showing that I am authentic and living with love, forgiveness, and understanding.

The life experience I have outlined in every chapter of this book has been the foundation for The Iron Goddess (theirongoddess.com), which is discussed at length in the previous chapter. At The Iron Goddess, we not only work on and challenge our fitness and nutrition, but we also work on resilience and what we call "the inner work confidence," which encompasses accountability, sexuality, spirituality, and mindset. In a nutshell, it encompasses our total belief system.

I encourage readers to know that every single aspect of our being contributes to our identity. And I don't care how old or young someone is. It is never ever too early or too late to find that iron goddess within. I've said this before, and I'm saying it again: the woman inside is a warrior who stands up for herself. She never allows anyone to treat her with anything less than respect and love. The iron goddess brand is a wild and powerful membership. It is sensual, and full of life, inspired by youth. An iron goddess has energy that's built on inspiration, resilience, optimism, and new habits. Using an integrated balance of scientific methods and life experience and education, I invite everyone to step into my membership and experience the iron goddess energy.

As an Iron Goddess, I pledge every day that I will:

Open my heart to love by speaking with integrity, honesty, respect, and kindness;

Fuel my body and brain with goodness by making healthy choices, like eating natural foods, moving my body how I desire, and being quiet through meditation or a walk in nature;

Commit to world class excellence and unshakable habits by setting intentions and following through with what I say I'm going to do;

Have gratitude and embrace challenges as they take me to new places that I may have never thought possible;

Allow the freedom I crave by saying yes to opportunities like travel, learning a new language, and seeing old friends or making new ones;

Forgive and lend a hand to others in need as we are all connected in this world.

In closing, I'd like to say that I am an IRON GODDESS, and as such, I know that I am not perfect. I will make mistakes. Change can be beautiful and messy. I am RESILIENT, I am EMPOWERED, I am COMMITTED. I LOVE MYSELF for exactly who I am right in this present moment.

With this new-found fierce freedom, I have discovered so many wonderful things about myself. One of the biggest changes in me has been that the negativity—both internal and external—has wreaked havoc on my sexuality, my worth, my boundaries, and my desires, so much so that I am now working on my next book, *The 8th Wonder of the World: The Female Orgasm*. I have opened up the floodgates, so to speak, with this newfound fierce freedom! XO Kathy